FROM LANDSCAPES TO LOTS: UNDERSTANDING AND MANAGING MIDWESTERN LANDSCAPE CHANGE

A PROGRESS REPORT

NORTH CENTRAL RESEARCH STATION
LANDSCAPE CHANGE INTEGRATED RESEARCH AND DEVELOPMENT PROGRAM

PAUL H. GOBSTER AND ROBERT G. HAIGHT
SCIENCE CO-LEADERS

Acknowledgments

The research findings described in this report stem from a sustained effort among Station scientists and collaborators since the inception of the Landscape Change Integrated Research and Development Program in 1998. Those playing a critical part in shaping the program included Tom Crow, Linda Donoghue, John Dwyer, Eric Gustafson, Bob Haack, Warren Heilman, Pam Jakes, Dennis May, Dave Shriner, Frank Thompson, and Mike Vasievich. Researchers contributing to the individual projects highlighted on these pages are cited in the text, with contact information and citations for further reading provided in appendix 1. A complete list of contributors to NCRS-sponsored landscape change studies is provided in appendix 2. We are grateful for their participation in the Landscape Change Program and for the opportunity to learn from them in our service as program co-leaders.

This report is dedicated to David S. Shriner (1945-2003), who as Supervisory Assistant Director of the Landscape Change Integrated Program provided a sustaining leadership and an endearing enthusiasm for landscape change research at the North Central Station.

North Central Research Station
U.S. Department of Agriculture - Forest Service
1992 Folwell Avenue
Saint Paul, Minnesota 55108
2004
www.ncrs.fs.fed.us

EXECUTIVE SUMMARY

This document is a progress report to stakeholders of the Landscape Change Integrated Research and Development Program, highlighting the results of research conducted during 1999-2003 to provide policy-relevant information about development-related landscape change in the seven-State Midwest region. Four questions are addressed:

How is the landscape changing? Our research has helped to identify the critical patterns and trends of changes in the Midwest region over recent decades. Detailed information on housing density and land cover and county data on forest characteristics, plants and animals, and human demographics have been organized in a Web-based atlas available to researchers, planners, and decisionmakers. Special studies on other critical patterns such as ozone concentrations help us understand trends and linkages within and beyond the region.

What drives landscape change? Physical, biological, social, and economic factors combine in complex ways to draw people to locations within the region not only to visit, but also increasingly to build primary residences and second homes. This amenity migration has traditionally centered on the riparian areas within the region but is increasingly spreading to forest and agricultural areas of the urban and rural fringe.

What are the consequences of landscape change? Forest parcelization and low-density development patterns are affecting the people and ecosystems of the region. At the urban fringe, fragmentation of forest cover is resulting in reductions in songbird populations and the decline in health of oak ecosystems. There also are concerns in more rural areas, such as economic impacts to the forest industry as increasing housing density results in fewer timber removals. Concerns about sprawl among metropolitan residents have increased across the Midwest region, with the perceived effects on environmental quality, farmland and open-space protection, traffic, and other problems varying in intensity from city to city.

What do we do about it? Strategies for avoiding, minimizing, or ameliorating the negative effects of landscape change include policies aimed at protecting open space by regulating land use, providing incentives to landowners and developers, and educating homeowners. The effectiveness of many open-space protection strategies has not been tested, but approaches that integrate multiple tools and authorities have the highest potential for succeeding. Understanding the goals of planners and residents can go far to achieve long-term, effective, and equitable guidelines for landscape change.

In the highlighted studies and in other efforts within and outside the region, the North Central Research Station is contributing to the knowledge base needed to discover, understand, and make reasoned decisions about development-related landscape change. Stakeholder participation is needed to help guide the future course of work in this critical area.

CONTENTS

From Landscapes to Lots: Understanding and Managing Midwestern Landscape Change

A Progress Report

Introduction

Contemporary patterns of population growth, landownership, and development are changing the landscape of urban, suburban, and rural areas throughout the United States. Population growth on the edges of metropolitan areas exceeded 10 percent in 1990-2000 as people continued to sprawl outward from large, densely settled urban cores (Heimlich and Anderson 2001) and rates of land conversion from open space to developed uses far exceeded rates of population growth (Fulton *et al.* 2001). One of the places where land consumption is most visible is the Chicago metropolitan area. During the 1990s, population growth in nine suburban counties (598,000 people, 25%) was more than twice the population growth in Cook County (281,000, 5.5%), which contains the city of Chicago (Johnson 2002), and land consumption in the region grew by 40 percent (Openlands Project 1999). In addition to the very rapid growth of metropolitan areas, population growth in non-metropolitan, recreation counties throughout the United States exceeded 20 percent in 1990-2000 as people migrated to and established residences in rural areas rich in natural amenities and other recreational attractions (Johnson and Beale 2002). In the northwoods of the Great Lakes States, population growth in 70 recreation counties exceeded 15 percent (Johnson and Beale 2002).

Although population growth often spurs positive economic changes such as more job opportunities, higher property values, and prosperity, it can have negative consequences for the area's social, physical, and biological systems. Stakeholders are concerned about:

- **Environmental degradation**—loss of biological diversity, increased forest fragmentation, reduced quality and quantity of wildlife habitat, reduced air and water quality.
- **Commodity production**—reduced availability of timber and mining resources, greater extraction costs, higher levels of conflict with adjacent landowners.
- **Community relations**—overcrowding, loss of unique identity and special places, increased conflicts between new and established residents, increased infrastructure costs and planning challenges.
- **Recreation quality**—loss of access to private land, loss of opportunities for solitude, increased conflicts between participants in new and established recreation activities.

Paul H. Gobster is a Research Social Scientist, with the North Central Research Station, Evanston, IL, and Robert G. Haight is a Research Forester with the North Central Research Station, St. Paul, MN.

In response to these concerns, scientists throughout the United States are studying the impacts of population growth and development in both metropolitan and rural areas. One of the most important landscape attributes affected by development is forest cover. Changes in species composition, size, shape, and spatial distribution of forest patches are related to the physical environment, ownership, and land use history (Crow et al. 1999). For example, roads fragment forests and reduce the amount of interior forest habitat (Miller et al. 1996). In suburban areas, housing fragments forests which contributes to a reduction in water quality (Wear et al. 1998) and degradation of wildlife habitat (Theobald et al. 1997). Similar effects occur as a result of low-density human development in rural areas. Since the 1940s, low-density housing dispersing outward from large urban centers has contributed to the fragmentation of forests in the St. Croix River valley of Minnesota and Wisconsin (Andersen et al. 1996). Forest fragmentation, in turn, can isolate plant and animal populations and threaten their existence (Saunders et al. 1991).

Increasing population and development can affect the sustainable forest productivity of a region. For example, researchers found that population density was a significant predictor of commercial timberland in five counties of western Virginia, and the probability of forest management decreased with increasing population and approached zero as population density exceeded 150 people per square mile (Wear et al. 1999). Working with data for Mississippi and Alabama, researchers found lower timber harvest rates in areas with higher population density (Barlow et al. 1998). These case studies highlight the need for further research on the impacts of increasing population and housing on the incidence of various kinds of timber harvest, harvest costs,

timber supply, and employment in the logging and wood processing sectors.

A great deal of thinking has gone into the factors that influence human settlement patterns, and current social trends suggest that environmental amenities are receiving more weight in individual location decisions (Stewart 2002). Retirement, technologies that facilitate working from a distance, disposable income, and second-home ownership are factors that influence migration decisions. As a result, people may be moving to non-metropolitan counties not because of better jobs and wages but because their lifestyle and wealth allow them to choose places with more environmental amenities. Given increased demand for housing in non-metropolitan counties, location of development depends on topographic features like slope and elevation and distances to major roads, metropolitan centers, and water (Turner et al. 1996, Wear and Bolstad 1998). Knowing where development is likely to occur allows us to evaluate potential environmental hazards and mitigation strategies.

There is a growing literature on alternative public policy tools for guiding development and mitigating its negative consequences (Fischel 1990, O'Neill 1999). One such tool is open-space protection. Government programs to protect open space grew in popularity in the 1990s with the passage of numerous State and local referenda, which raised billions of dollars for acquiring privately owned open space (Hollis and Fulton 2002). Although designated open spaces protect natural areas and provide opportunities for recreation and education, they affect housing prices and the pattern of development (Riddel 2001). Thus, decisions to increase the amount of public conservation land should depend not only on the environmental and amenity benefits but also on the housing and employment impacts to surrounding communities (Lewis et al. 2002).

The work described above and much more forms a solid foundation for addressing problems specific to the Midwest region, with its complexity of forest types, landforms, people, and land uses. Merging our disciplinary capacities in landscape and wildlife ecology, forest inventory and analysis, social sciences and economics, meteorology, and other areas, the North Central Research Station launched the Landscape Change Integrated Research and Development Program in 1998 (Gobster et al. 2000). The program is aimed at tackling key problems and issues concerning the development-related aspects of landscape change. Teams of scientists from various disciplines are working together on common problems, many for the first time. Focusing on our seven-State region (fig. 1), we hope to provide the specific information that forest managers and policymakers need for guiding growth and change in the Midwest and to transfer that information elsewhere when possible.

Purpose and Objectives of the Landscape Change Integrated Program

The purpose of the Landscape Change Integrated Program is to combine the efforts of scientists across the Station's research work units to develop a better understanding of land use and land cover change and to develop knowledge and tools to help people make informed choices about how they use natural resources. Based on a series of workshops and other communications with researchers and stakeholders, we identified four overarching objectives to:

1. Characterize the current patterns of land use and land cover change in the Midwest region.
2. Understand the physical, biological, social, and economic factors influencing the rate and extent of landscape change.

3. Determine the effects of landscape change on people and ecosystems.
4. Assess the effectiveness of public policies for regulating landscape change.

Scope of this Document

This document describes research findings, policy implications, and tools that we have developed during the program's first 5 years (1999-2003) to help people make informed choices about their natural resources.

Consistent with the program's objectives, this report provides information relevant to the discussion of four main questions:

1. How is the landscape changing?
2. What drives landscape change?
3. What are the consequences of landscape change?
4. What do we do about it?

Our findings focus on landscape change issues in the seven States of the Midwest region (fig. 1). These issues are associated with migration and settlement patterns of people across an urban to rural gradient and the impacts of those patterns on our region's natural resources.

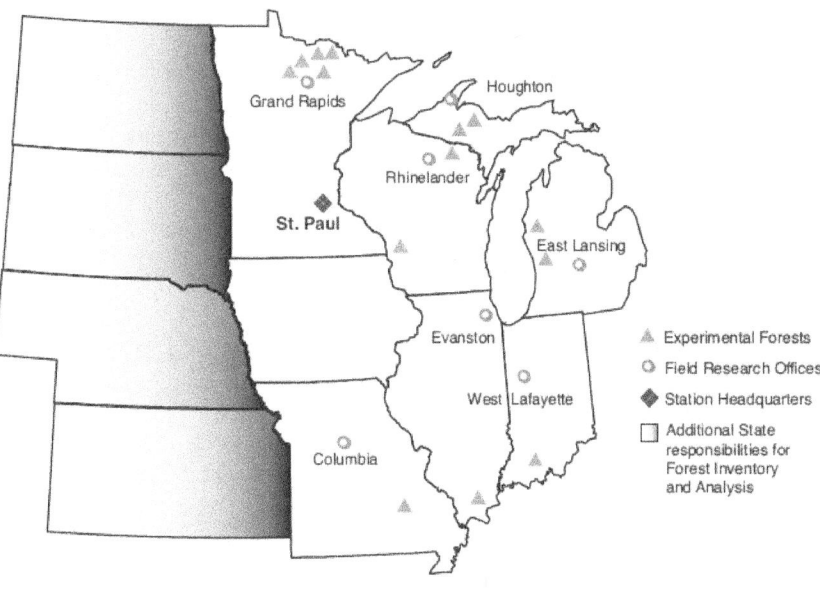

Figure 1.—*The seven-State region of the North Central Research Station.*

LITERATURE CITED

Andersen, O.; Crow, T.R.; Lietz, S.M.; Stearns, F. 1996.
Transformation of a landscape in the upper mid-west, USA: the history of the lower St. Croix River Valley, 1830 to present. Landscape and Urban Planning. 35: 247-267.

Barlow, S.A.; Munn, I.A.; Cleaves, D.A.; Evans, D.L. 1998.
The effect of urban sprawl on timber harvesting: a look at two southern states. Journal of Forestry. 96(12): 10-14.

Crow, T.R.; Host, G.E.; Mladenoff, D.J. 1999.
Ownership and ecosystem as sources of spatial heterogeneity in a forested landscape, Wisconsin, USA. Landscape Ecology. 14: 449-463.

Fischel, W.A. 1990.
Do growth controls matter? A review of empirical evidence on the effectiveness and efficiency of local government land use regulations. Cambridge, MA: Lincoln Institute of Land Policy. 68 p.

Fulton, W.; Pendall, R.; Nguyen, M.; Harrison, A. 2001.
Who sprawls most? How growth patterns differ across the U.S. Washington, DC: The Brookings Institution Center on Urban and Metropolitan Policy. 24 p.

Gobster, P.H.; Haight, R.G.; Shriner, D. 2000.
Landscape change in the Midwest: an integrated research and development program. Journal of Forestry. 98(3): 9-14.

Heimlich, R.E.; Anderson, W.D. 2001.
Development at the urban fringe and beyond: impacts on agriculture and rural land. Agric. Econ. Rep. 803. Washington, DC: U.S. Department of Agriculture, Economic Research Service. 80 p.

Hollis, L.E.; Fulton, W. 2002.
Open space protection: conservation meets growth management. Washington, DC: The Brookings Institution Center on Urban and Metropolitan Policy. 84 p.

Johnson, K.M. 2002.
The changing face of Chicago: demographic trends in the 1990s. Chicago Fed Letter #176, April. Chicago, IL: Federal Reserve Bank of Chicago. 4 p.

Johnson, K.M.; Beale, C.L. 2002.
Nonmetro recreation counties: their identification and rapid growth. Rural America. 17(4): 12-19.

Lewis, D.J.; Hunt, G.L.; Plantinga, A.J. 2002.
Public conservation land and employment growth in the northern forest region. Land Economics. 78: 245-259.

Miller, J.R.; Joyce, L.A.; Knight, R.L.; King, R.M. 1996.
Forest roads and landscape structure in the southern Rocky Mountains. Landscape Ecology. 11: 115-127.

O'Neill, D. 1999.
Smart growth: myth and fact. Washington DC: Urban Land Institute. 26 p.

Openlands Project. 1999.
Under pressure: land consumption in the Chicago region 1998-2028. Chicago, IL: 31 p.

Riddel, M. 2001.
A dynamic approach to estimating hedonic prices for environmental goods: an application to open space purchase. Land Economics. 77: 494-512.

Stewart, S.I. 2002.
Amenity migration. In: Luft, K.; MacDonald, S., comps. Trends 2000: shaping the future, 5th Outdoor recreation & tourism trends symposium; 2000 September 17-20; Lansing, MI: Michigan State University, Department of Park, Recreation and Tourism Resources: 369-378.

Saunders, D.A.; Hobbs, R.J.; Margules, C.R. 1991.
Biological consequences of ecosystem fragmentation: a review. Conservation Biology. 5: 18-32.

Theobald, D.M.; Miller, J.R.; Hobbs, N.T. 1997.
Estimating the cumulative effects of development on wildlife habitat. Landscape and Urban Planning. 39: 25-36.

Turner, M.G.; Wear, D.N.; Flamm, R.O. 1996.
Land ownership and land-cover change in the Southern Appalachian Highlands and the Olympic Peninsula. Ecological Applications. 6: 1150-1172.

Wear, D.N.; Bolstad, P. 1998.
Land-use changes in Southern Appalachian landscapes: spatial analysis and forecast evaluation. Ecosystems. 1: 575-594.

Wear, D.N.; Turner, M.G.; Naiman, R.J. 1998.
Land cover along an urban-rural gradient: implications for water quality. Ecological Applications. 8: 619-630.

Wear, D.N.; Liu, R.; Foreman, J.M.; Sheffield, R.M. 1999.
The effects of population growth on timber management and inventories in Virginia. Forest Ecology and Management. 118: 107-115.

How is the Landscape Changing?

Human-influenced changes in the landscape can vary widely. Some are sudden and localized, such as the removal of timber from a woodlot, while others like global climate change can be imperceptibly slow and widespread. Identifying the key *patterns* of landscape change in the Midwest region is thus an essential first step in understanding what potential impacts such changes can have and ultimately what to do about them. To help answer questions about how the landscape is changing, we have begun to identify important physical, biological, and social patterns in the landscape at the regional or subregional scale—ecological land types, forest cover, land use, population densities, and other factors. Using a diverse set of data from the Forest Inventory and Analysis program, the U.S. Census Bureau, satellite imagery, and other sources, we are putting together a region-wide picture of landscape patterns. To enrich this base of data, we have also conducted expert and media analyses to help identify the types of issues resonating with stakeholders at specific places within the region. As the following research highlights demonstrate, we now have a solid understanding of the location, magnitude, and rate of change and their manifestations in the landscape.

The Changing Midwest: An Atlas of Landscape Change

"If a picture is worth a thousand words, then a map is worth a thousand pictures." This geographer's adage recognizes the value maps have in revealing important spatial relationships about people and resources that are often not visible from the ground. Maps of landscape change add another valuable dimension—a temporal one—and can thus reveal critical patterns of how our landscape is evolving over space and time by providing information about the concentration and dispersion of people and resources, rates of change, and other important clues about what is happening to the landscape in which we live.

NCRS researchers Rob Potts and Eric Gustafson visualized these patterns of change across the Midwest region as an important first step in developing hypotheses about the causes and consequence of development-related change and investigating strategies aimed at minimizing its negative effects. Working as part of an interdisciplinary team of researchers from the natural and social sciences, they developed a set of maps showing key aspects of change across the seven-State Midwest region. Sociodemographic and biophysical features are mapped at the county level for 1980 and 2000, and a third composite map shows the degree of change that occurred between these two periods.

The researchers mapped change in four broad sections of interest. The **Land Cover** section describes changes in the amount and distribution of the major land cover types in the region (i.e., Agriculture, Forestland, and Urban). The **Forest Characteristics** section provides a comprehensive account of change in forests by forest type group, including change in area, volume, structure, composition, and ownership (e.g., fig. 2). The **Plants and Animals** section describes change in the relative abundance of species of special concern. And the **Human Demographics** section describes change in population, housing and seasonal housing density, and personal income.

The Changing Midwest is available in atlas form and on the NC Web site: http://www. ncrs.fs.fed.us/IntegratedPrograms/lc/. The set of maps lays the groundwork for subsequent studies that will examine the interactions between people and resources across the region, such as a state-by-state identification of hotspots of land cover change (see inset). The set also is intended for use by planners and others who need broad coverage of key indicators of change at the State and regional levels. Perhaps its highest and best use, however, will be to show citizens and policymakers where we have gone as a region over the last two decades and to stimulate discussion about the future.

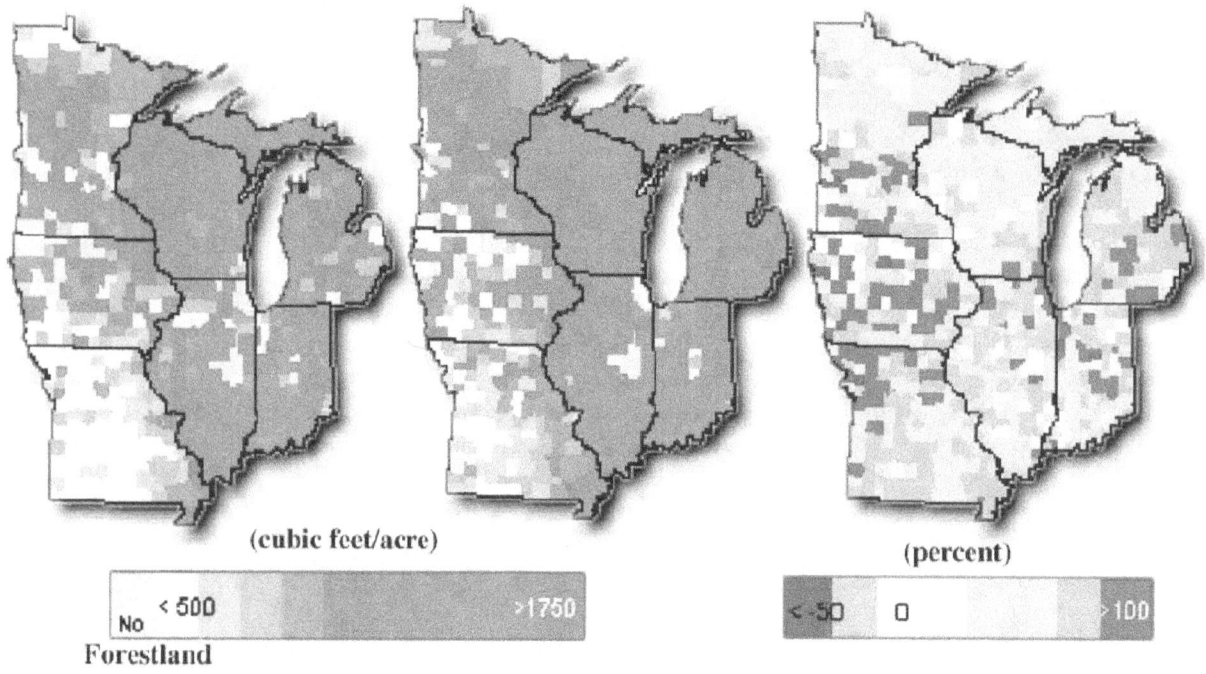

(cubic feet/acre)

No Forestland   < 500   >1750

(percent)

< -50   0   >100

Figure 2.—Percent change in the volume of all growing-stock trees, all ownerships, 1980-2000.

Planner's Toolkit: Mapping the Hotspots of Landscape Change

One illustration of the utility of the Changing Midwest Landscape assessment is a Web-based slide show depicting land cover change. Region-wide, three trends in land cover change emerged between 1980 and 2000:

- Low change—The corn and soybean belts in Illinois and Iowa, and forestland in northern Minnesota, Wisconsin, and Michigan remained relatively stable.

- Medium change—Productive and marginally productive agriculture experienced moderate levels of change. Productive agriculture near high-tech areas tended to convert to urban. Marginally productive agriculture tended to revert to forestland.

- High change—Urban and suburban areas associated with large cities experienced significant change, particularly along major rail and water routes.

The slide show depicts hotspots of change in each of the seven States in the Region. Within a given State, users can select from a list of city names to view hotspots of rapid land cover change, as well as areas of low or medium change. Maps and data tables provide land cover change information over the two decades.

Patterns of Housing Density Change Across the Midwest Region, 1940-2000

Of all the patterns of development-related change that occur in the landscape, the distribution of people is perhaps the most revealing. Where people choose to live can provide clues to the resources and other factors that are driving landscape change and can foreshadow where and to what extent we might expect changes that will impact the landscapes we value. In this respect, housing density is a particularly important measure of population distribution because it can be used to examine the spread of development in urban and rural areas, and to show to what extent forests and other open lands are becoming fragmented.

As an extension of the Changing Midwest assessment just described, NCRS social scientist Susan Stewart has been working with demographer Roger Hammer and landscape ecologist Volker Radeloff of the University of Wisconsin-Madison to chart changes in housing density across the Midwest region. The team has developed new demographic methods that make it possible to reconstruct past patterns of residential density as well as to project them into the future.

Maps of the 1940-2000 housing density patterns for the region (fig. 3) show that growth is impacting urban, suburban, and rural areas alike. Across the seven-State region the number of housing units more than doubled from 1940 to 2000, with mid-level housing densities increasing the most in area. Low-density development started to become widespread in the forested rural and exurban regions of northern Minnesota, Michigan, and Wisconsin, and southern Missouri during the 1970s, and more than two-thirds of all Midwest forests contained at least four housing units/km^2 by 2000. Although major urban centers grew little after the 1940s, their associated suburban areas continued to grow throughout the period. By contrast, most

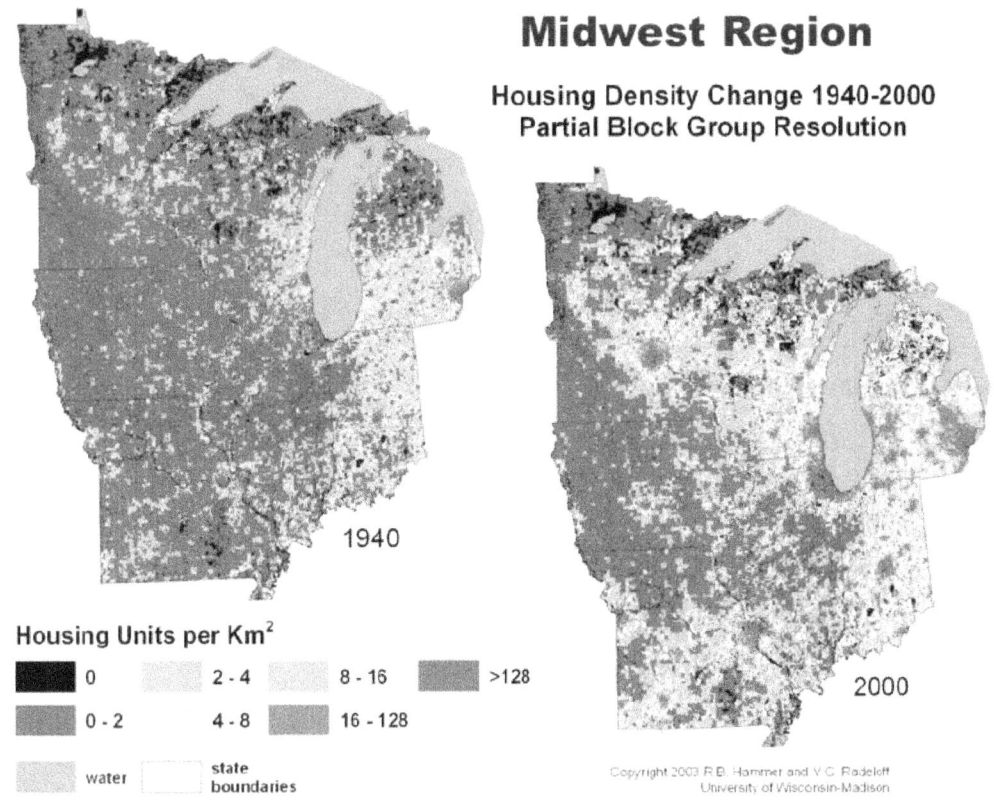

Midwest Region

Housing Density Change 1940-2000
Partial Block Group Resolution

1940

2000

Housing Units per Km^2

0	2 - 4
0 - 2	4 - 8
	8 - 16
	16 - 128
	>128
water	state boundaries

Figure 3.—Housing density change in the Midwest region, 1940-2000, partial block group resolution.

smaller cities, towns, and rural areas in the Midwest region's farm belt grew slowly or not at all over these five decades.

Going beyond the detail needed for the assessment, the housing density maps are accurate enough to use in resource management and landscape ecological research. When combined with land cover information, the maps are enabling the research team to identify where land fragmentation is occurring as well as to examine potential impacts to wildlife, increases in fire risk, and other resource management concerns. The housing density maps are available at http://www.ncrs.fs.fed.us/IntegratedPrograms/lc/

Land Cover Change in the Midwest Region

A second key extension of the Changing Midwest assessment has been to understand in a more detailed way how land cover in the Midwest region is changing. Remotely sensed data, including aerial photography and satellite imagery, can provide the level of detail needed by natural resource scientists, planners, and managers to do their jobs more efficiently and accurately. But until recently, the lack of comparable data sets has prevented these groups from using remotely sensed data to detect how landscapes change over time.

To remedy this problem NCRS scientist Rob Potts has worked with researchers Daniel Brown and Kathleen Bergen of the University of Michigan to develop new methods for merging disparate sets of remotely sensed land cover data. In so doing, they produced a classification system that permits them to detect changes in land cover at a resolution of 1 km with an accuracy rate of more than 90 percent.

Applying this methodology to the seven-State Midwest region, the researchers have given us a comprehensive picture of land cover change between 1980 and 2000 (fig. 4). They found that the most common types of landscape change were from agriculture to forestland and from agriculture to urban. Specifically, the area of forestland in the Midwest region increased by 18.7 percent (about 12.5 million acres), and the area of urban lands increased by 23.4 percent (about 1.4 million acres).

This improved ability to use remotely sensed data to detect landscape change puts researchers, planners, and managers in a better position to understand the forces that are driving change, as well as the ecological, economic, and social consequences of change. In other words, it gives us the data we need to understand the effects of landscape change on plants, animals, and water.

Remotely sensed data, including aerial photography and satellite imagery, can provide the level of detail needed by natural resource scientists, planners, and managers to do their jobs more efficiently and accurately.

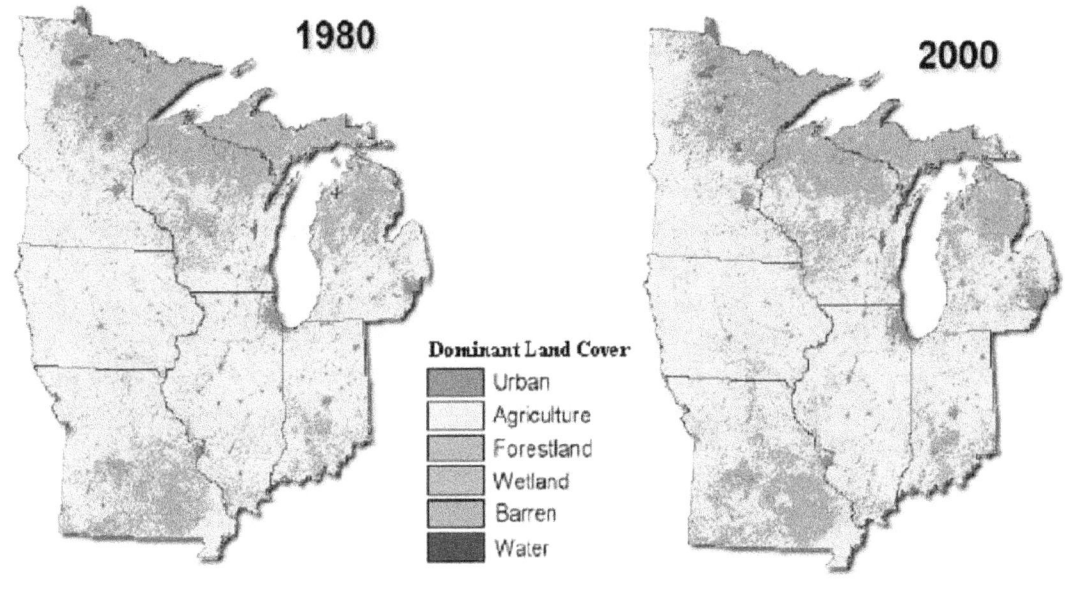

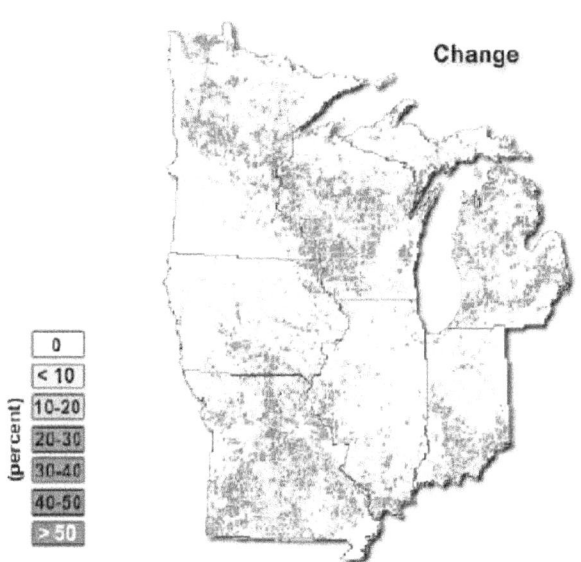

Figure 4.—*Forestlands increased by 12.5 million acres between 1980 and 2000, predominantly in less productive agricultural areas of the region.*

Dynamics of Ozone in the Western Great Lakes Region

The way we live can both directly and indirectly impact the natural resources we value. As the population of the Midwest region grows, development is not only consuming progressively larger areas of open space, but it is also increasing the number of miles we have to drive during a day also thereby increasing air pollution. Ozone (O_3) is one component of air pollution that significantly threatens not only human health but also the health and productivity of forest ecosystems. Understanding the patterns of O_3 generation and movement is thus particularly important in predicting pollution impacts to the Midwest region and beyond. Ozone generated in the atmosphere through chemical reactions can be transported great distances by atmospheric winds, and the weather and climate conditions that control O_3 formation and its transport can be influenced by landscape factors such as urban and suburban development, road usage, land usage, bodies of water, topography, and vegetation patterns.

Because O_3 pollution is a regional problem, land use decisions and policies related to urban and suburban development and transportation network usage in one area can impact O_3 pollution in other distant areas.

To get a handle on these complex patterns, NCRS scientist Warren Heilman worked with Jerome Fast of the U.S. Department of Energy—Battelle Pacific Northwest National Laboratory to simulate O_3 formation and transport over the western Great Lakes region (e.g., fig. 5). Using a coupled weather and atmospheric chemistry model, their simulations for a 30-day period during the summer of 1999 revealed the following six findings.

(1) Ozone produced in one area of the Great Lakes region can affect O_3 concentrations in other areas on subsequent days. For example, O_3 produced in Illinois and Wisconsin can be transported into southern Canada and the northeastern U.S. (2) High surface O_3 concentrations are frequently produced over the Great Lakes surfaces, even when atmospheric conditions over land are not conducive to O_3 production. (3) Ozone production over the Great Lakes is very sensitive to lake temperatures. (4) Reducing the emission rates of oxides of nitrogen leads to higher O_3 concentrations over southern Lake Michigan immediately downwind of Chicago and Milwaukee, and lower O_3 concentrations in more remote areas. (5) Increases in the emission rates of oxides of nitrogen *and* volatile organic compounds lead to higher O_3 concentrations downwind. (6) Ozone concentrations in remote rural and forested areas of the region will increase if current population growth patterns continue.

These findings suggest that natural resource managers, when predicting future forest health conditions in the western Great Lakes region, should take into account the potential impact of future O_3 pollution patterns resulting from regional landscape and climate changes. Because O_3 pollution is a regional problem, land use decisions and policies related to urban and suburban development and transportation network usage in one area can impact O_3 pollution in other distant areas. In addition, air quality regulators and policymakers in the Great Lakes region should consider the cumulative effects of altered Great Lakes water temperatures and future changes in land usage when developing O_3 pollution standards and assessing future impacts.

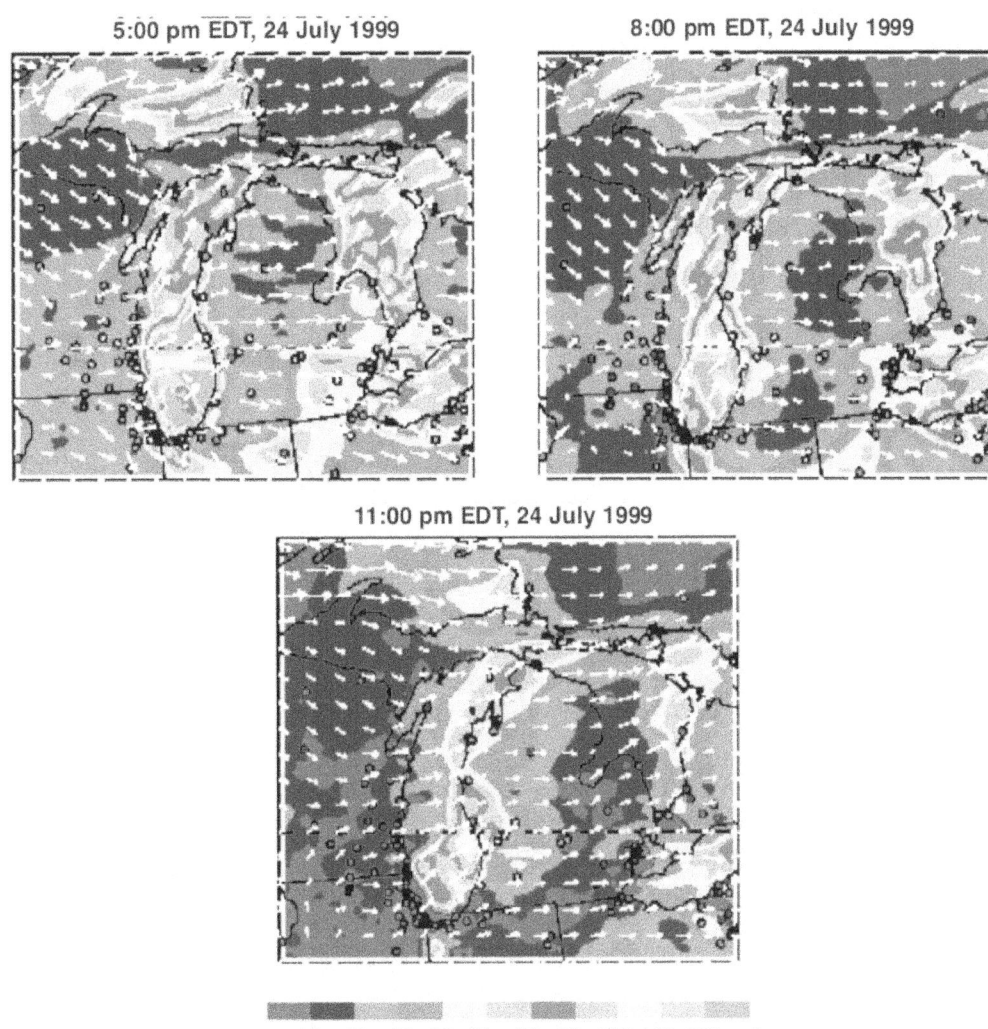

5:00 pm EDT, 24 July 1999   8:00 pm EDT, 24 July 1999

11:00 pm EDT, 24 July 1999

30 40 50 60 70 80 90 100 110 120 ppb

Figure 5.—Observed (dots) and simulated (contours) surface O_3 concentrations in parts per billion (ppb) at 5:00 pm EDT, 8:00 pm EDT, and 11:00 pm EDT on 24 July 1999 over the western Great Lakes region. Wind vectors in white show the direction and relative speed of surface winds. The figures indicate (1) maximum surface O_3 concentrations typically occur over the Great Lakes, (2) O_3 can be transported over large distances, and (3) high surface O_3 concentrations can occur in remote areas of the region, far from the major urban centers where O_3-producing chemicals from sources are emitted into the atmosphere.

WHAT DRIVES LANDSCAPE CHANGE?

Since the 1970s, one of the most important features of the changing midwestern landscape is the movement of people into forested rural and exurban regions of northern Minnesota, Michigan, and Wisconsin and southern Missouri. The high rates of rural in-migration throughout the 1970s declined sharply in the 1980s but increased again in the 1990s across the majority of rural counties in the region. And some rural counties were bypassed by this urban to rural migration.

The most compelling explanation for the rural renaissance is that people want to live in areas rich in natural resource amenities and are willing to sacrifice higher wages, better job opportunities, and urban amenities for a better quality of life. Many aspects of the way we live in America in the 21st century make amenity migration possible. The Baby Boom generation is approaching retirement age. Portable pensions and dispersed families make retirement migration easier than it was for earlier generations. Moving to a small town, perhaps where they grew up or where they have vacationed or owned a second home, is an attractive option. Among working age people, a growing number have no one place that constitutes being "at work," instead telecommuting or traveling extensively. New communication technologies also make working from a home office easier.

Scientists at the North Central Research Station are leading an effort to understand the role of natural resources and the increasing diversity of social factors influencing urban to rural migration. The three studies in this section describe the importance of forests, lakes, and, surprisingly, roads, in people's decisions to move to rural areas or commuter-based subdivisions outside cities. Amenity migration is a trend worth watching because it can bring major, fundamental change to the social and natural landscape.

Amenity Migration as a Driver of Landscape Change

People are moving to the countryside in increasing numbers and accepting longer commutes in order to live near forests, lakes, and streams. These amenity resources have always drawn visitors and seasonal homeowners, but recent shifts in patterns of work make it easier than ever for people to make these special places their permanent home.

Susan Stewart, social scientist from NCRS's Evanston unit on urban populations and the natural environment, working with Loyola University-Chicago demographer Kenneth Johnson, found evidence of amenity migration in county population changes in the U.S. Census. Non-metropolitan counties throughout the U.S. with recreational attributes such as national forests had higher population growth rates between 1990 and 2000 than those without such amenities. Recreational counties grew by 20.2 percent between 1990 and 2000 compared to 10.4 percent for non-metropolitan counties as a whole and 13.2 percent for all U.S. counties. Migration, not natural increase (more births than deaths), was the demographic driver of most of this growth.

The striking difference in growth between counties with and without amenity resources suggests that we should pay close attention to demographic changes in places where natural resources attract new residents. Walworth County, Wisconsin, is such a place. Situated in a rolling countryside with lakes, small towns, and farms, Walworth County is within a 2-hour drive for the 10 million people of the Chicago and Milwaukee metropolitan areas.

The attractive nature of Walworth County is reflected by its 25-percent population gain between 1990 and 2000.

To find out more about amenity migration, Susan Stewart and Kenneth Johnson studied this hotspot of non-metropolitan growth. The researchers surveyed more than 500 residents of households owning residential property close to one of 12 lakes in Walworth County. Sixty-two percent of the respondents were second home owners, who also owned homes in the Chicago metropolitan area (fig. 6). Many residents said that Walworth County's proximity to Chicago and Milwaukee was a key factor in their decision to purchase their home. Both second-home owners and permanent residents were also attracted by the recreational and scenic amenities of the area. Residents and second-home owners both make extensive use of the lakes and recreational amenities, and both groups strongly support efforts to preserve the environmental quality of the area. Second-home owners also contribute significantly to the local economy. Spending on their second homes averages $13,005 per year, exclusive of mortgage payments, and they use their second home an average of 97 days a year. Nearly 40 percent of the second-home owners plan to become permanent residents of the area in the future.

The changing community composition can affect attitudes toward the environment, willingness to engage in civic organizations, and recreational use of forests.

Population increases around our national forests and other rural amenity areas can increase pressure on recreational facilities and local services. In addition, migration can change the age structure, ethnic mix, minority concentrations, education, and income of a county's population over a very short time. The changing community composition can affect attitudes toward the environment, willingness to engage in civic organizations, and recreational use of forests. Continued attention to the changing *size* and demographic *structure* of populations in areas important to the Forest Service can help managers and policymakers understand social change and anticipate which counties need particular care in planning and management.

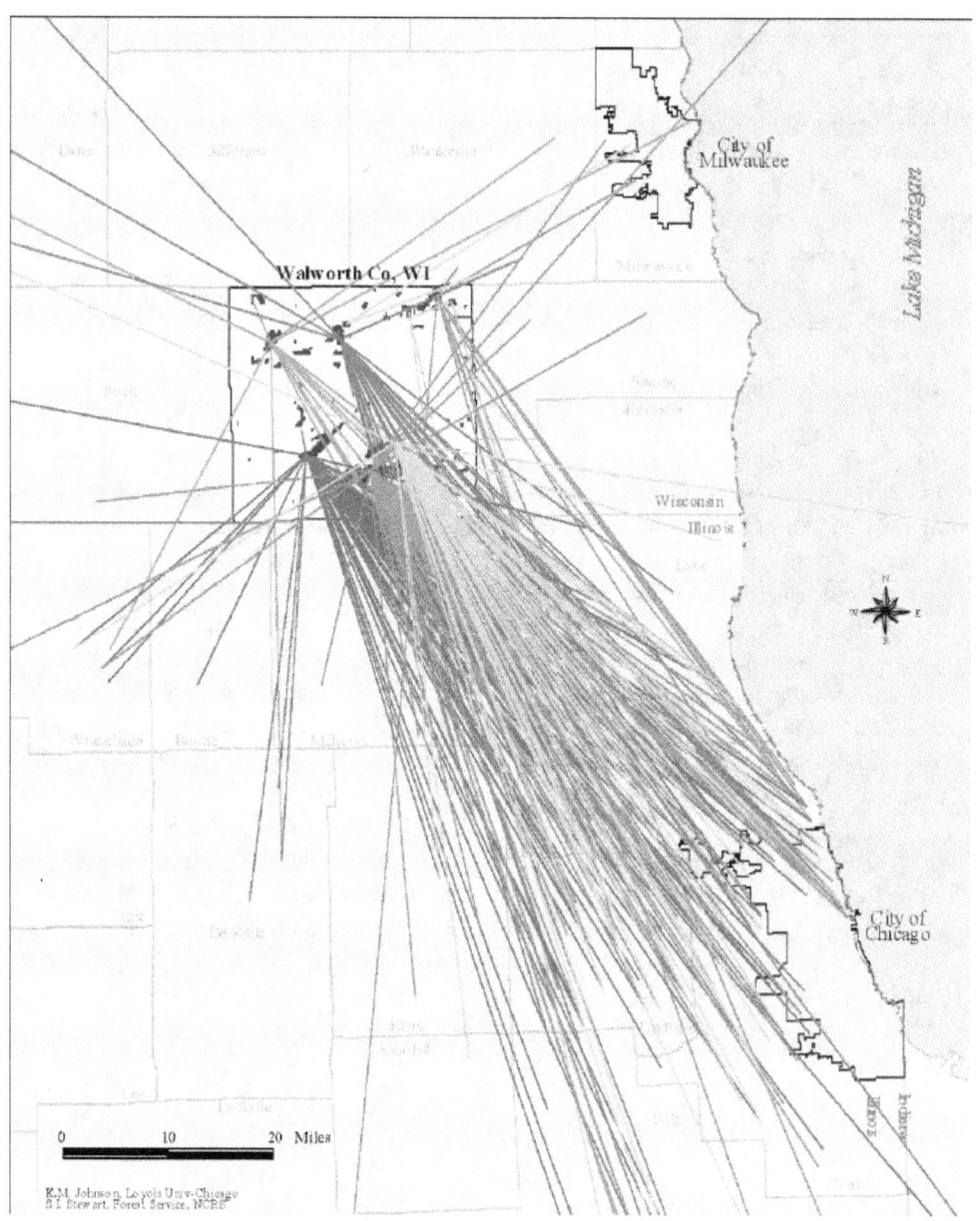

Figure 6.—*Primary residences of Walworth County second home owners.*

Accessibility as a Driver of Landscape Change

Parcelization (land ownership fragmentation) and development of private forestlands can have major repercussions for economic, ecological, and quality of life values and thus have become critical concerns of many individuals, public agencies, and private groups across the United States.

To better understand these concerns, NCRS social scientist Paul Gobster and University of Wisconsin-Madison forestry professor and extension specialist Mark Rickenbach studied stakeholders who attended a series of discussion forums about parcelization and development held across northern Wisconsin. Participants generally saw the greatest change occurring near the outskirts of towns and cities and around traditional amenity areas. However, they were often surprised at new patterns of seasonal home development occurring on forestlands away from water and permanent homes well beyond common commuting distances. People felt that recent highway improvements reduced daily and weekend commuting distances and thus put formerly unconsidered areas on the market. Although improvement and expansion of roads aimed to reduce congestion, they also improved accessibility and increased the potential for parcelization and development of private forestlands, especially those near favored recreation areas.

In a related study of the drivers of parcelization, Station scientists Paul Gobster and Tom Schmidt looked broadly at factors thought to be influencing private forestland parcelization across the northern Lake States using FIA data from the last two forest inventory cycles. Using stand area as an indicator of parcel size, they found proximity of forestlands to water bodies and roads showed the strongest relationships to changes in parcel size. Furthermore, some of the greatest changes in parcel size were happening in the smallest ownership class, 0-10 acres (fig. 7). These findings suggest private forestlands accessible and close to recreation areas are being subdivided into parcels of a size that may be valued more for their use as home sites than for their potential for wildlife habitat or timber harvesting.

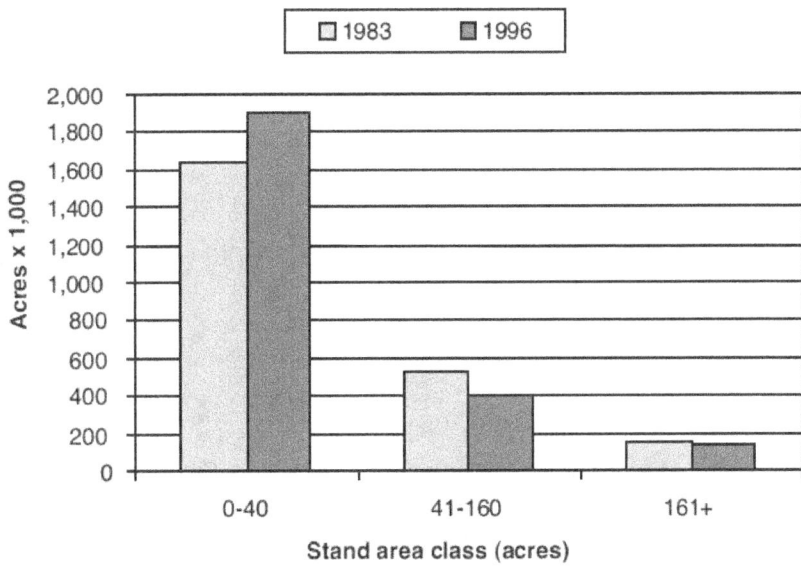

Figure 7.—*Changes in parcelization of private timberlands in northwest Wisconsin, 1983-1996. Source: North Central Research Station FIA Statistics (see Gobster and Schmidt 2000).*

Figure 8.—*Subdivision at the forest fringe.*

Homeowners' and Developers' Views of Nature

Home buyers are flocking to new residential developments at the rural fringe of many metropolitan areas (fig. 8). Among the appeals of living "out in the country" are "being closer to nature" and "having space." To find out what these concepts mean to new homeowners, NC's Evanston unit worked with University of Michigan social scientists Rachel Kaplan and Maureen Austin to interview individuals who purchased homes in new conservation-based subdivisions in southeast Michigan. Residents' satisfaction with their communities was overwhelmingly influenced by the **availability of forests, wetlands, and open meadows.** People who owned homes in subdivisions with smaller lots set around a commonly held and managed natural area were pleased with their **access to nearby nature.** However, they varied considerably in their understanding of the reasons for open-space conservation surrounding their housing development. Some fully understood the conservation intent of their subdivision, while others did not understand it at all.

This range in understanding could undermine conservation outcomes because if people are not aware that they are at least partly responsible for the remaining open space, they could make choices that threaten the long-term health of that open space.

The provision of conservation-based housing alternatives is closely related to homeowners' preferences and demands. Thus, to complete the picture, the Evanston unit worked with Michigan State University social scientist Karen Vigmostad to find out how real estate developers viewed nature in the context of their work. In interviews with prominent developers in Michigan, several key issues emerged. **Development *is* and *is not* about money**—although successful developers were largely profit oriented, they also held altruistic goals of "building neighborhoods" and helping people's dreams come true. **Nature is invisible**—developers for the most part have little awareness of nature and wildlife unless these values are protected by law or public interest. **The market drives development**—most developers contend that the demand for single family detached homes on large lots is still by far the norm and feel no particular responsibility to try to change people's preferences. **Planning and regulation are key**—developers may resent new environmental controls but will work within and may even be creatively stimulated by measures to protect natural values as long as they are applied equitably to all developers.

These findings suggest important guidelines for policymakers. **Provide homeowners with better information about open-space conservation design**, which may lead them to more fully appreciate their access to nature and continued involvement in managing local natural areas. **Provide planners and developers with better information about ecology**—handbooks and coursework could increase awareness about natural area protection, particularly if such information were tied to incentive programs. **Make planning part of the solution, not part of the problem**—master plans and ordinances often make it difficult for developers to protect natural values. Plans must be examined and revised to accommodate more ecologically sensitive development alternatives. **Channel developers' creativity and passion in positive ways**—allowing higher building densities and other types of incentives in exchange for conservation-oriented designs can challenge developers to seek creative ideas for developing new property. These positive incentives may be preferable to heaping additional regulations upon the development process, which often leads to homogeneity and minimum standards of compliance.

This range in understanding could undermine conservation outcomes because if people are not aware that they are at least partly responsible for the remaining open space, they could make choices that threaten the long-term health of that open space.

WHAT ARE THE CONSEQUENCES OF LANDSCAPE CHANGE?

Development-related landscape change can affect people and ecosystems in many ways. Some of the consequences of change can be positive; in a recent study about private forestland parcelization and development in northern Wisconsin, stakeholders participating in discussion forums said that increased fragmentation of forest cover could increase some desired types of wildlife, particularly edge species, and that human population increases have expanded the range of goods and services available in some rural communities. Most participants, however, felt the negative impacts of change were far more pervasive than the positive ones. In that study and others conducted over the last 5 years, we have begun to systematically document and quantify how development-related changes are affecting the people and ecosystems of the Midwest region. In the following sections, we highlight four studies that illuminate the consequences of change within and across the region.

Effects of Urbanization on Songbird Populations

Urbanization can significantly threaten valued songbird species, according to a new field study based in and around Columbia, Missouri. In the research, NCRS scientist Frank Thompson teamed up with University of Missouri ecologist Dirk Burhans to isolate the effects of urbanization on songbird populations. The researchers compared old-field sites in the city of Columbia with similar rural sites in nearby Boone County, conducting population counts; examining nest predation by songbird enemies such as snakes, raccoons, and house cats; and investigating incidents of brood parasitism by brown-headed cowbirds.

After collecting and analyzing three breeding seasons of data, the researchers concluded that floodplain fields of similar size and structure may contain very different songbird communities due to urbanization. Although they found no differences in the level of nest predation between the two landscapes, the populations of some songbirds such as the blue-winged warbler, white-eyed vireo, and field sparrow common to the rural sites were rarely or never detected in bird counts at the urban sites. Urban populations of brown-headed cowbirds, on the other hand, were significantly greater than at the rural sites. The

researchers suspect that the urban landscape may especially favor cowbirds, in turn putting songbirds at a disadvantage. Because cowbirds feed heavily at bird feeders and forage in short-grass habitats such as lawns, urbanized settings may constitute cowbird-rich habitats that are not beneficial to songbirds during the portion of the breeding season in which cowbirds are active. With their abundance in urban areas thus assured, cowbirds can further harm urban songbird populations through brood parasitism, a phenomenon where cowbirds lay their eggs in the nests of songbirds, who then hatch the intruding chicks while often losing their own. Here, the researchers' findings were especially conclusive. For three species common to both urban and rural landscapes, the northern cardinal, indigo bunting (fig. 9), and yellow-breasted chat, the researchers found that nests were parasitized 3 to 12 times more frequently in the urban landscape (fig. 10).

Figure 9.—*Indigo bunting, a neotropical songbird on the decline in urbanizing areas of the Midwest region.*

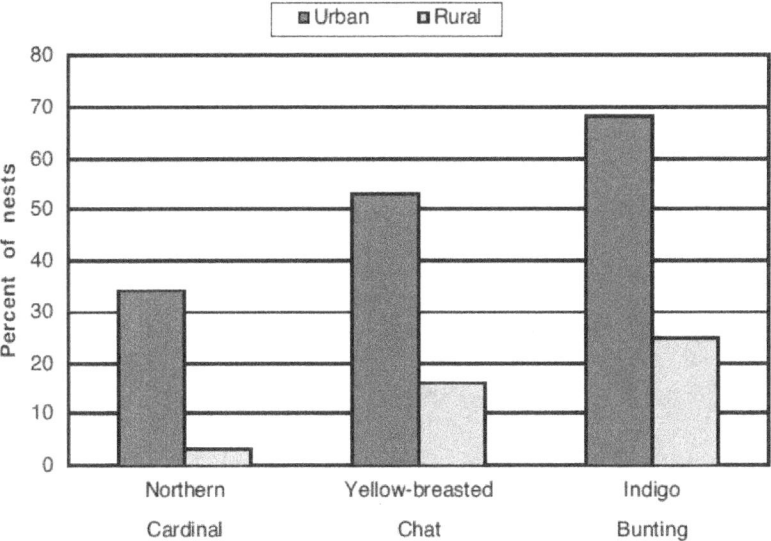

Percent of nests parasitized by brown-headed cowbirds according to landscape type

Figure 10.—*Songbirds were parasitized by cowbirds 3 to 12 times more frequently on urban study sites than on similar sites in rural areas.*

The researchers' findings take on a greater sense of urgency when looked at in the broader context of development-related landscape change. The Columbia metropolitan area grew significantly over the period 1982-1997, with a rate of land conversion to urbanized uses (47%) nearly double that of human population growth (25%). Like many places across the Midwest region, development was greatest at Columbia's metropolitan fringe, with Boone County, the location of the study's "rural" sites, receiving the majority of the region's building permits for new housing. Thus, without any change in development trends, the researchers' findings suggest that songbird populations will likely continue to decline as urbanization increases in the region. The impact of this loss could have economic as well as ecological repercussions for the region. Recent data from the USDA Forest Service's National Survey on Recreation and the Environment show that birdwatching is the Nation's fastest growing recreational activity, participated in by nearly 70 million Americans and a favorite among aging Baby Boomers with high discretionary income. In this respect, the findings of this study warn that birdwatching opportunities will decline in quality and quantity with the onset of urbanization, particularly at the urban fringe nearest to where most people live.

Effects of Housing Density on Timber Harvesting

As shown in previous chapters on the patterns and drivers of landscape change, housing density in rural and amenity areas of the Midwest region has increased significantly in recent years. Researchers who have identified this phenomenon are now beginning to assess the potential impacts it might have on the social, economic, and biological assets of the region. In one such study, University of Wisconsin-Madison Ph.D. student Alexia Sabor is quantifying how housing density may be affecting the timber resource and economy of the Upper Great Lakes States. Working with NCRS social scientist Susan Stewart and UW-Madison researchers Volker Radeloff and Roger Hammer, Sabor and her team have combined Forest Inventory and Analysis (FIA) and U.S. Census data to examine the relationships between housing density, timber removals, and mortality of forests in Michigan, Minnesota, and Wisconsin.

By calculating the density of houses at various distances from FIA plots, the researchers found that timber removals decreased substantially as housing density increased. Results show that less than 10 percent of harvesting events occur in areas where housing density exceeds 20 units per km² (fig. 11).

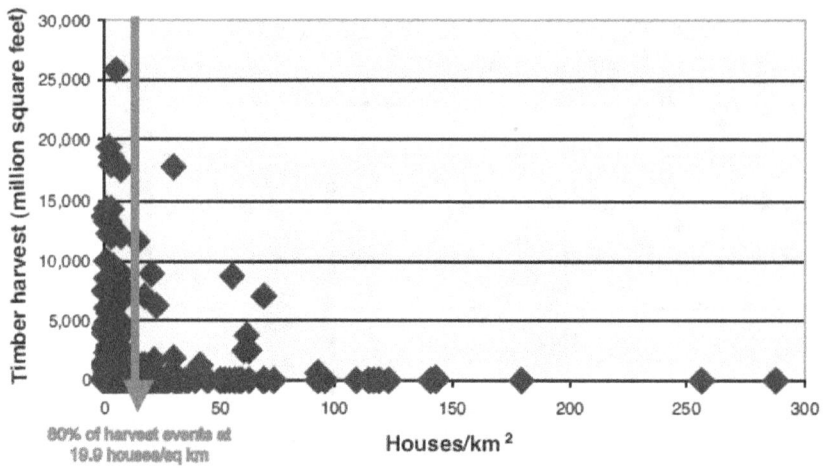

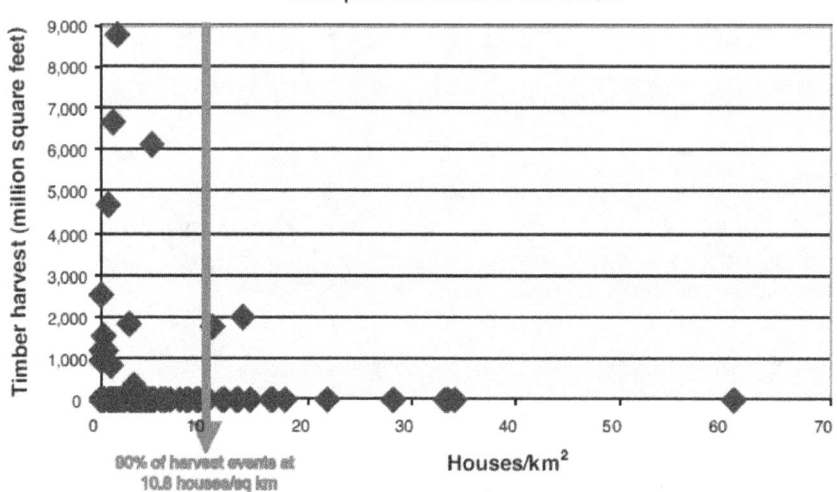

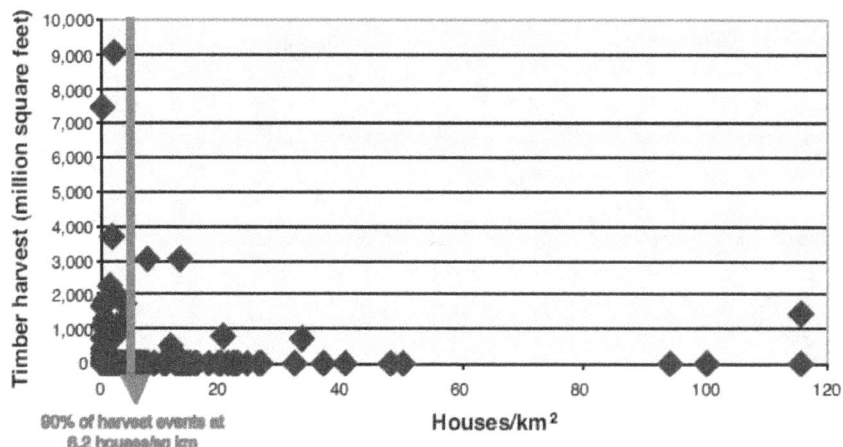

Figure 11.—*The sensitivity of timber harvesting to housing density is shown for three different timber types. In all cases, less than 10 percent of harvesting occurs in areas where housing density exceeds 20 units per km².*

These results suggest timber harvesting rates are closely related to housing density, even in areas relatively sparsely populated. In addition, the researchers found mortality significantly decreased as housing density increased.

The research team suspects these relationships may be due to an increased resistance to timber management as private nonindustrial forestlands are subdivided and developed for second homes. These new owners focus primarily on the recreational and esthetic values of their land and are not likely to see timber harvesting as a compatible objective. Because the demand for second homes is expected to rise, these results indicate timber harvesting in the Upper Great Lakes States may decrease significantly in the coming decades.

Protecting the Health of Oak Forests in Urbanizing Landscapes

Oak ecosystems formed the original landscape matrix for what have since become the largest urban centers of the Midwest region—St. Louis, Kansas City, Indianapolis, Detroit, Chicago, Milwaukee, and Minneapolis-St. Paul. With growth and development, however, these ecosystems have been so radically altered and transformed within these metropolitan areas that today they exist only as remnant patches rather than as large contiguous areas. In many cases, significant patches in the form of woodlots and riparian zones still exist at the urban fringe, but are often unprotected and threatened by development.

How can our metropolitan areas continue to grow and prosper yet maintain and protect these heritage oak landscapes? NCRS scientist Jennifer Juzwik is working with a team of researchers from the North Central Station and the University of Minnesota to find out. Their focus is the Minneapolis-St. Paul metropolitan area, a seven-county, 2,800 mi² region currently home to more than 2.6 million people. Echoing a pattern seen across the region, Minneapolis-St. Paul's 25 percent growth in population from 1982 to 1997 was dwarfed by a more than 60 percent increase in developed land area.

Looking at broad changes in the region with the help of multi-temporal satellite imagery (Landsat TM), the research team found the area of oak forest in the region decreased by 4 percent between 1991 and 1998 (fig. 12). The number of individual oak forest patches also decreased, as did the average patch size in six of seven ecological subsections in the region. Decreases in oak acreage during this period were highly correlated with increases in three indicators of urbanization: population density, impervious surface area, and developed land area (fig. 12). In 75 percent of the cases where oak stands were completely removed, the stands had been located close to roads and lakes.

With growth and development, however, these ecosystems have been so radically altered and transformed within these metropolitan areas that today they exist only as remnant patches rather than as large contiguous areas.

In a followup study at a finer scale, the researchers found differences in oak loss were related to land use class, with the greatest losses (75%) found in Medium Density Residential and Commercial-Retail-Office classes (fig. 13). Moderate and low oak acreage losses were found in Low Density Residential and Rural Residential classes, respectively. Declines in forest health were related also to land use class (fig. 13). Looking at changes in the spectral reflectance from satellite images taken of the sites in 1991 and 2000 as a measure of changes in forest health, the researchers found the greatest reductions in health for sites in the Medium Density Residential class.

The team is now working to develop a predictive model to estimate future oak losses across the metro region for the next 20 years based on land use class. This information will be of interest to regional, county, and community managers and planners as well as natural resource specialists in the region. As team members continue to develop their base of knowledge, they hope to work with these individuals and groups in developing best management practices to maintain and protect the oak resource in our region's metropolitan areas.

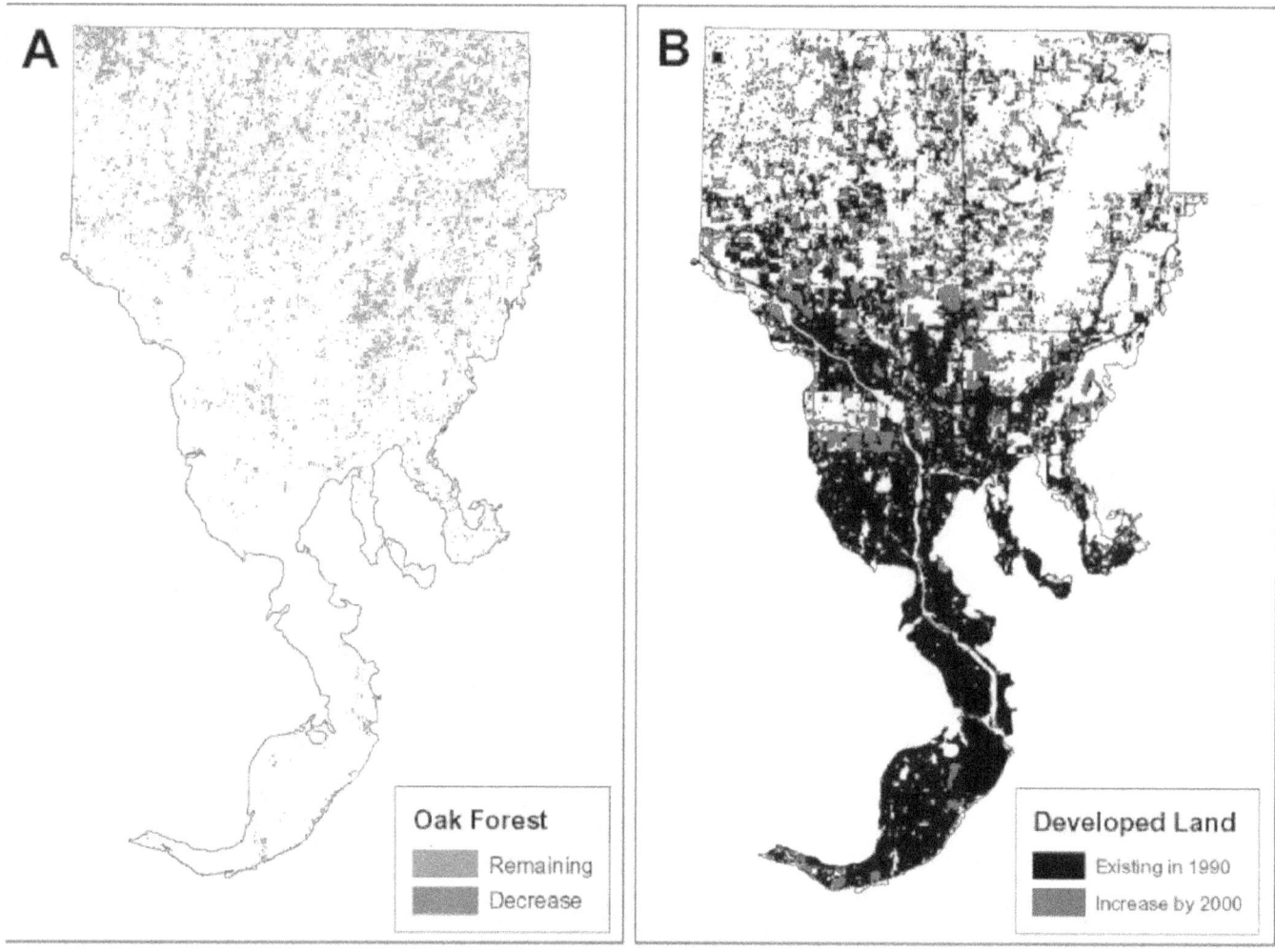

Figure 12.—(A) Decrease in oak forest in Anoka Sand Plains subsection from 1991 to 1998, (B) Increase in developed land in Anoka Sand Plains subsection from 1990 to 2000.

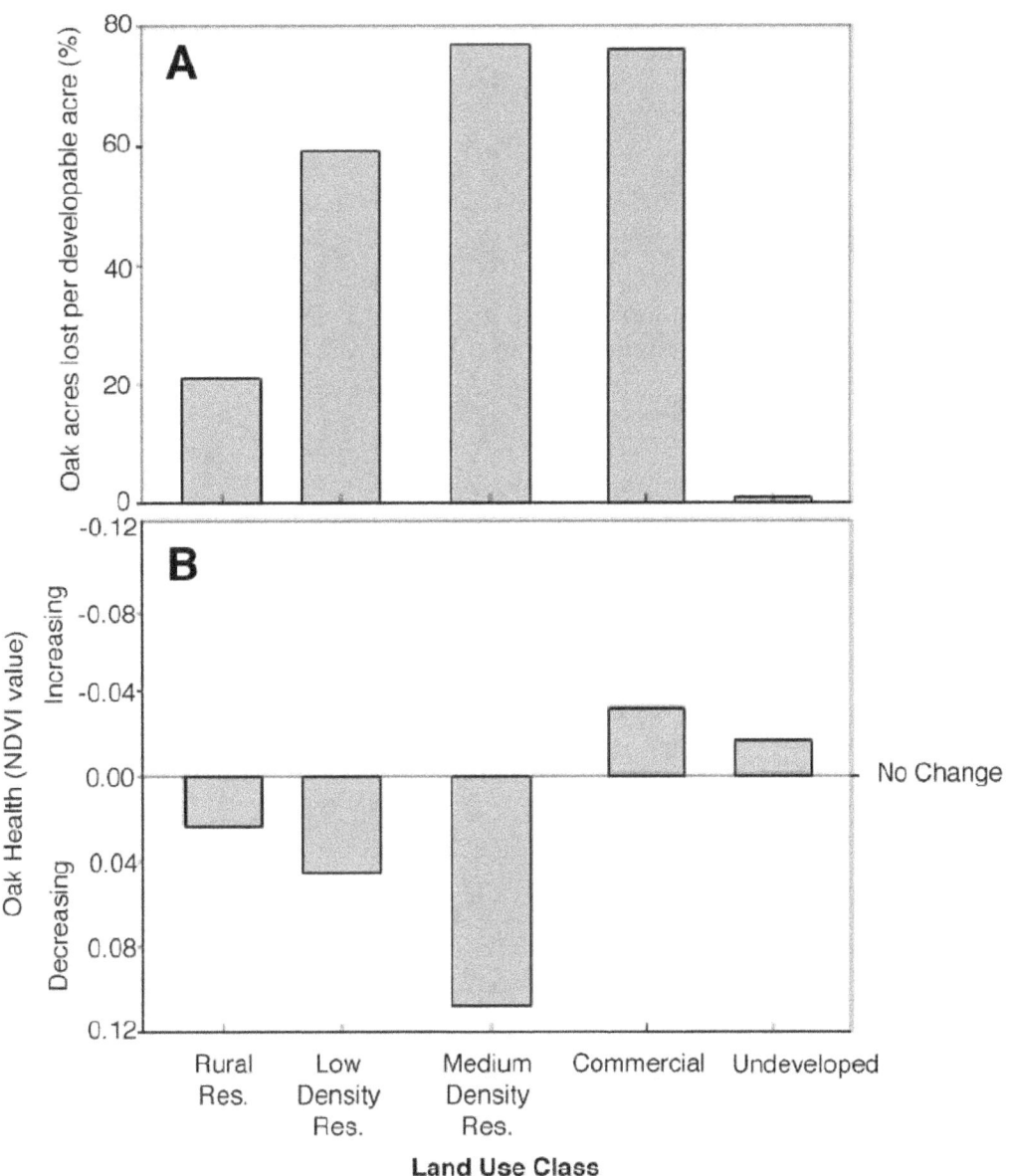

Figure 13.—(A) Oak forest loss (%) from 1991 to 2000 in five land use classes, (B) Oak forest health change from 1991 to 2000 in five land use classes.

Planner's Toolkit: A Multimedia CD on Oak Wilt Management

Oak wilt is a severe fungal infection, endemic to Eastern and Midwestern States, that kills red oaks swiftly and white oaks more slowly, often over several seasons. It is a big problem, killing thousands of trees every year and destroying oaks highly prized as shade trees.

In an effort to combat its spread, Jennifer Juzwik, a research plant pathologist and project leader for North Central's Forest Diseases Research Unit, led a team in the development of a multimedia CD entitled *Oak Wilt: People and Trees—a Community Approach to Management.* Released in July 2003, the CD uses Microsoft PowerPoint presentations, videos, and PDF documents to outline prevention and treatment strategies that can halt the spread of oak wilt in a variety of settings, from backyard trees to urban forests and beyond.

The CD's target audiences include urban and community foresters, city administrators, tree inspectors, parks and recreation staff, and anyone else interested in an integrated oak wilt management program.

The CD contains three PowerPoint presentations. The first explains the details of the disease, including a description of it, a guide to identifying it, an explanation of how it spreads, an overview of management techniques, and an almanac of treatments over the year. For example, summer is the best time for surveying for disease and administering fungicides, while fall is a good time to use the deep plows to sever root grafts between neighboring trees, a key route of disease transmission. Another presentation goes over a variety of oak diseases that look similar to oak wilt. And the third presentation illustrates several management challenges and intervention strategies, most centered around different approaches to severing root grafts. The presentations include links to 30- to 90-second videos that illustrate key points. The presentations and video files are easily accessible to the average reader with little or no knowledge of tree pests and are brief enough the entire contents of the CD can be viewed in less than an hour.

For those who want more indepth information, the CD also includes a number of PDFs of Federal and State brochures that go into much greater detail on specific topics. One, entitled *How to Identify, Prevent, and Control Oak Wilt,* is an electronic version of a Forest Service brochure that describes in well-illustrated detail the disease cycle, symptoms, distribution, and management techniques. Another is a guide to identification of the sap beetles that spread oak wilt. Others include instructions for collecting field samples for testing and a guide for homebuilders working in wooded lots, which is important because trees wounded by construction are particularly susceptible to infection.

Also included in the CD are public domain versions of viewing software to ensure the user can view the contents.

The CD is available from the North Central Research Station and the Northeastern Area, State and Private Forestry units, of the USDA Forest Service.

The Perceived Impacts of Urban Sprawl Across Thirteen Midwestern Cities

Various indicators point to an increase in concern about the environmental and social costs associated with sprawling development patterns. But these indicators are quite broad, typically covering large geographic areas (such as attitude surveys of the entire Nation) and including only general concerns about sprawl. This type of information is too broad to inform policymaking and management in specific areas.

To provide more geographically sensitive information about the perceived impacts of sprawl, NCRS scientists David Bengston and Rob Potts collaborated with media analyst David Fan of InfoTrend, Inc., to monitor the salience of key sprawl-related issues for 13 metropolitan areas in the Midwest region from 1995 to 2000. The study provides a new approach for the continuous monitoring and assessment of a broad range of trends in public concerns, attitudes, beliefs, and values.

The researchers found eight main concerns about urban sprawl. In order of their importance across the United States, these included concern about (1) environmental impacts (such as loss of wildlife habitat, forest fragmentation, decreased air and water quality), (2) loss of farmland, (3) loss of open space, (4) traffic congestion, (5) urban decline (the concern that sprawl contributes to the decline of core cities as public resources are dedicated to growth at the periphery instead of redevelopment and revitalization of urban centers), (6) taxpayer subsidies (the concern that sprawl does not pay its own way and is subsidized by taxpayers), (7) loss of a sense of community, and (8) loss of historic sites (including historic buildings and districts, prehistoric sites, and so on). They also found an overall increase in these concerns about sprawl across the United States and in most metropolitan areas from 1995 to 2001.

This rising concern about the impacts of urban sprawl indicates there will likely be strong public support for growth management programs and efforts to protect open space.

Figures 14 and 15 illustrate findings for two metropolitan areas in the Midwest region. Figure 14 shows the overall and specific concerns about sprawl in Chicago. Concern about the impact of sprawl on traffic congestion was second most important in Chicago, typical of large metropolitan areas. Figure 15 illustrates the overall and specific concerns about sprawl in Des Moines. In contrast to Chicago, this figure shows loss of farmland was the number one concern about sprawl in Des Moines.

This rising concern about the impacts of urban sprawl indicates there will likely be strong public support for growth management programs and efforts to protect open space. More specifically, the researchers' finding that environmental impacts, loss of farmland, and loss of open space are the top three concerns about sprawl implies there may be strong support for public policies such as conservation easements, purchase of development rights, transfer of development rights, use-value taxation for resource lands, and other public policy instruments for protecting natural resources from development. Their findings for individual metropolitan areas provide insights into the specific concerns in those communities and guidance for the appropriate public policy response to address the concerns.

Overall sprawl concern, Chicago, IL

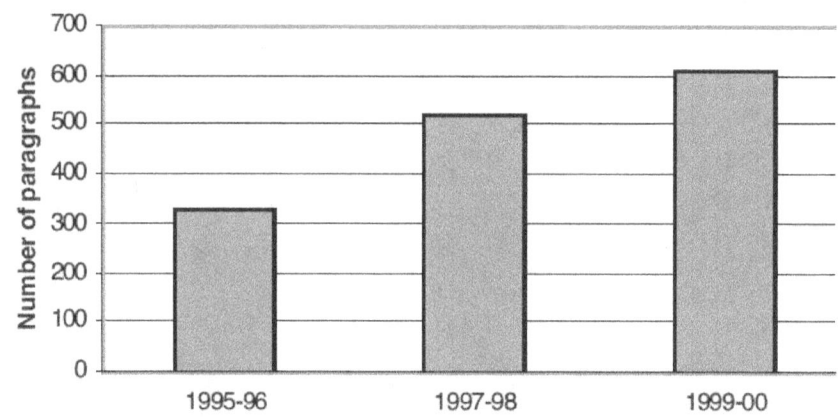

Specific sprawl concerns, Chicago, IL

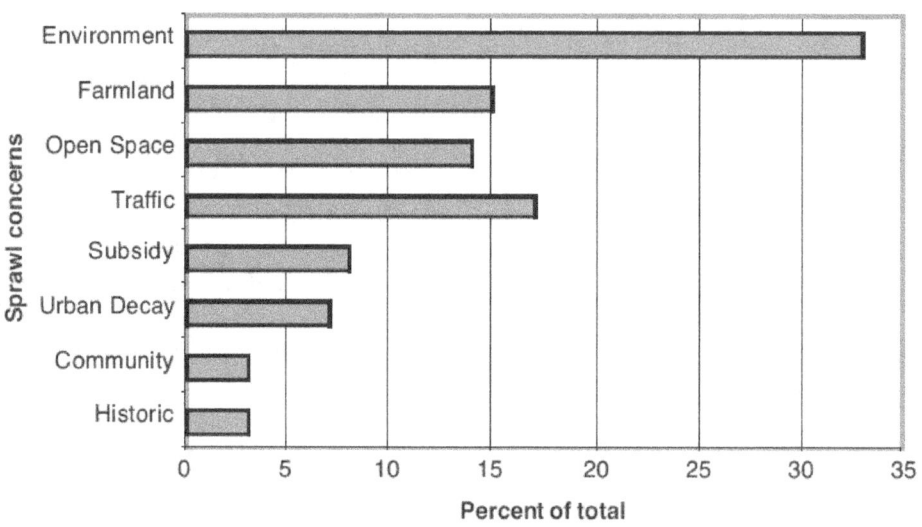

Figure 14.—*Overall and specific concerns about sprawl in Chicago.*

Overall sprawl concern, Des Moines, IA

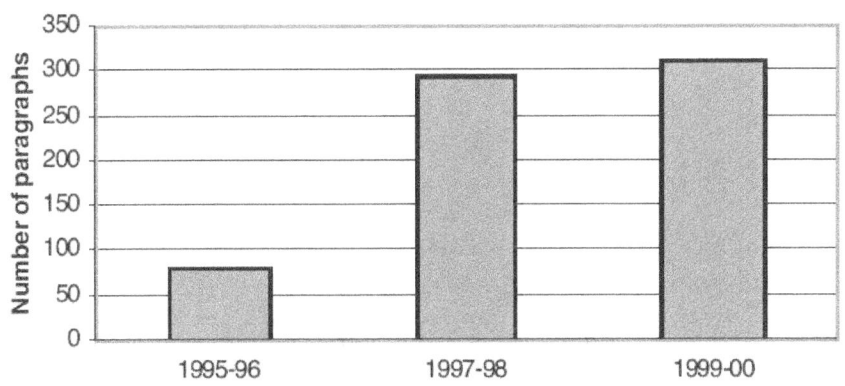

Specific sprawl concerns, Des Moines, IA

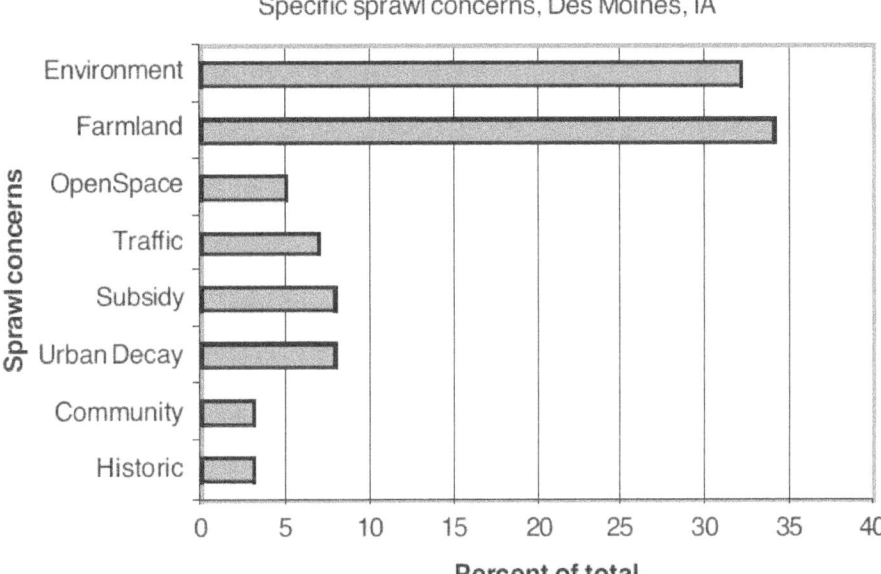

Figure 15.—*Overall and specific concerns about sprawl in Des Moines.*

WHAT DO WE DO ABOUT LANDSCAPE CHANGE?

The public sector in the United States has responded to growing concern about the social and environmental costs of sprawling development patterns by creating a wide range of policy instruments designed to manage urban growth and protect open space. A panoply of techniques has been implemented at the local, regional, State, and to a limited extent, national levels. Three broad categories of these policy instruments are *land acquisition, regulations* (e.g., development moratoria, adequate public facility ordinances, upzoning, urban growth boundaries, urban service boundaries, cluster zoning, exclusive agricultural or forestry zoning), and *incentives* (e.g., infill and redevelopment incentives, split-rate property tax, right-to-farm laws, transfer of development rights, purchase of development rights, use-value taxation). Scientists at the North Central Research Station are beginning to study these approaches to managing urban growth, including the process of land acquisition and protection, the potential impacts of land protection on spatial pattern of development, and the benefits of open-space neighborhoods.

One of the lessons learned from evaluating growth management policies is that active and meaningful participation by stakeholders throughout the process of planning and implementation is a cornerstone of effective growth management. One way to foster participation within a community is to understand residents' views about their environment. NCRS researchers are leading an effort to identify community identities and understand how they help form a shared vision of protecting valued places in the face of landscape change.

Public Policies for Managing Urban Growth and Protecting Open Space

Faced with growing populations and increasingly land-consumptive development, local, regional, and State governments in the United States are designing and implementing strategies to manage urban growth and protect open space (table 1).

To better understand the range of public policy options, David Bengston from the North Central Research Station, along with Jenna Fletcher of the Minnesota Forest Resources Council and Kristen Nelson of the University of Minnesota, systematically reviewed the extensive literature describing three broad categories of policy instruments: land acquisition, land use regulation, and incentive-based approaches.

The following key lessons were gleaned from the literature on the implementation and evaluation of growth management policies and programs. (1) Surprisingly few empirical evaluations of the effectiveness of growth management policies and programs have been carried out, despite decades of implementation of such policies and programs. (2) Administrative efficiency and other details of policy implementation—rather than the general type of policy—are critical in determining effectiveness. Poorly administered growth management policies often frustrate desirable development and make a community unattractive to developers. The result may be development leapfrogging to distant communities at higher environmental and social costs, exactly the opposite of what growth management seeks to achieve. (3) Multiple, reinforcing policy instruments are needed to increase effectiveness and avoid unintended consequences. For example, in the absence of zoning and other techniques to protect open space, purchase of development rights or conservation easements will likely result in a patchwork of protected lands that will be a magnet for development on unprotected adjacent lands. (4) Vertical coordination (between growth management policies at different governmental levels) and horizontal coordination (among neighboring communities, regions, or States) are critical for successful growth management but are often inadequate or lacking. (5) Active and meaningful participation by stakeholders throughout planning and implementation is a cornerstone of effective growth management.

Bengston and his colleagues conclude with a discussion of potential Federal roles in managing urban growth and protecting open space. Potential roles include helping to increase State and local planning capacity; coordinating local, regional, and State efforts; coordinating Federal development activities and growth management goals; and providing greater funding of incentives for open-space protection and infill development.

Table 1.—*Public policies for managing urban growth and protecting open space; the level of government at which they are typically applied is indicated in parentheses*

Policies for Managing Urban Growth	**Public Acquisition**
	Public ownership of parks, recreation areas, forests, wildlife refuges, wilderness areas, environmentally sensitive areas, greenways, and so on (local, regional, State, national)
	Regulation
	Development moratoria, interim development regulations (local)
	Rate of growth controls, growth-phasing regulations (local)
	Adequate public facility ordinances (local, State)
	Upzoning or small-lot zoning, minimum density zoning (local)
	Greenbelts (local, regional)
	Urban growth boundaries (local, regional, State)
	Urban service boundaries (local, regional)
	Planning mandates (regional, State)
	Incentives
	Development impact fees (local)
	Development impact taxes, real estate transfer taxes (local)
	Infill and redevelopment incentives (local, State)
	Split-rate property tax (local)
	Brownfields redevelopment (local, State, national)
	Location efficient mortgages (local)
	Historic rehabilitation tax credits (State, national)
Protecting Open Space	**Public Acquisition**
	Public ownership of parks, recreation areas, forests, wildlife refuges, wilderness areas, environmentally sensitive areas, greenways, and so on (local, regional, State, national)
	Regulation
	Subdivision exactions (local)
	Cluster zoning (local, regional)—incentives also sometimes used
	Downzoning or large-lot zoning (local)
	Exclusive agricultural or forestry zoning (local, State)
	Mitigation ordinances and banking (local, State)
	Nontransitional zoning (local)
	Concentrating rural development (local)
	Incentives
	Right-to-farm laws (local, State)
	Agricultural districts (local, regional, State)
	Transfer of development rights (local, regional)
	Purchase of development rights, conservation easements (local, State, Federal)
	Use-value tax assessment (State, national)
	Circuit breaker tax relief credits (State)
	Capital gains tax on land sales (State)

Goal Tradeoffs in Metropolitan Open-Space Protection

Major metropolitan areas in the United States are growing very rapidly, which has resulted in high rates of conversion of natural areas and open space in and around urban centers. In response, people are concerned that open spaces and the natural communities and recreational opportunities they sustain are being degraded or destroyed. These concerns are reflected in a resurgence of land protection activities by public agencies, non-profit groups, and local land trusts.

One of the places where the countervailing forces of land consumption and land protection are most visible is the Chicago metropolitan area. During 1990-1996, the metropolitan population grew by 9 percent while land consumption grew by 40 percent. This rapid rate of land consumption coincided with the passage of numerous county bond referenda in which funds were raised to acquire and preserve open space.

One of the places where the countervailing forces of land consumption and land protection are most visible is the Chicago metropolitan area.

To better understand land protection goals and process, Paul Gobster and Robert Haight from the North Central Research Station, along with University of Minnesota economists Jane Ruliffson and Frances Homans, interviewed 15 planners in municipal, county, regional, and State agencies and non-governmental organizations involved in open-space protection in the Chicago area. Although a wide variety of land protection organizations operate in Chicago, most of the land protection is done at the county level by county forest preserve districts, which can levy property taxes to acquire, restore, and protect natural areas.

Since 1995, over $450 million has been raised by forest preserve districts for new land acquisition. An important objective of land preservation planners is site accessibility: the provision of public access for passive recreation. Groups with the most money to spend on land protection are government agencies, who must argue their case to the public when persuading them to approve bond referenda. Public access is a powerful public relations tool because constituents can see the direct benefits of their financial contributions through their ability to use and enjoy a site. Another important goal is biodiversity conservation, including protection of native terrestrial communities, habitat for an endangered species, and large areas of high-quality habitat.

The research team developed a decision support tool that allows decisionmakers to discover tradeoffs between their land protection goals. For example, cost curves show how much area must be protected to increase the number of cities with access to protected sites (fig. 16). The cost curves show that, when land protection funds are limited, there can be a sharp tradeoff between the goals maximizing site accessibility and those maximizing species representation. The conflict can be reduced by protecting a larger number of small and relatively inexpensive reserves dispersed around the study area.

These results have important implications for planners and the general public. In the Chicago area, people who want to influence land protection decisions should work with county forest preserve district planners because they have the most funding available for land protection. Because the land area available for protection is shrinking, planners should seek to protect areas that provide multiple benefits, such as accessible recreational opportunities and protection of rare species and ecosystems.

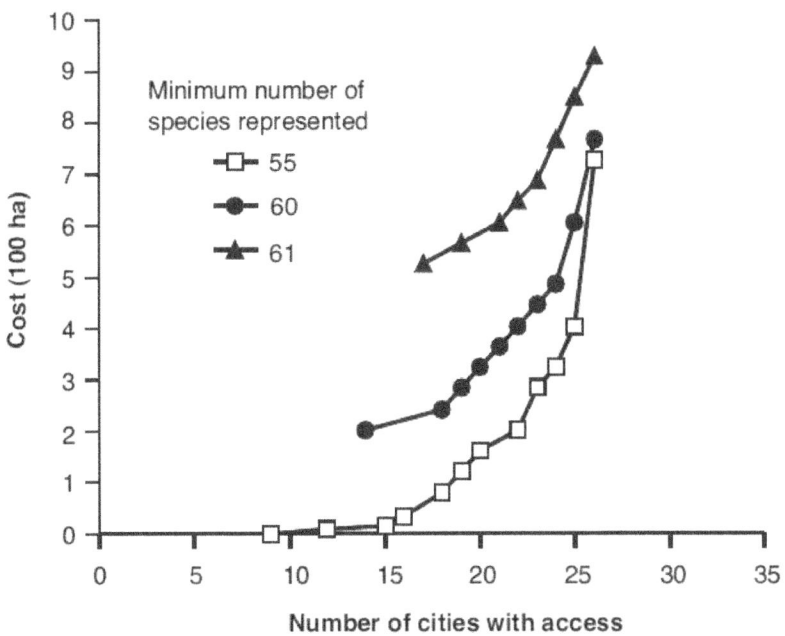

Figure 16.—*Cost curves showing gain in number of cities with access to protected sites for increasing cost (expressed in hectares protected) under different requirements for the number of species represented. A city has access if it has at least two protected sites within 3 km.*

Impacts of Open-Space Protection on Development Pattern

In the face of rapid housing and commercial development, planners in local and regional governments aim to protect open space for ecological, recreational, and esthetic purposes. Although protecting open space conserves natural resources and provides recreation services, it can also affect the spatial pattern of development, density of development, and property values both locally and regionally (fig. 17).

To understand the development impacts of open-space protection, Robert Haight from the North Central Research Station, along with University of Minnesota economists Liaila Tajibaeva and Stephen Polasky, developed a model of the housing market in an urban area with discrete neighborhoods and open space. Neighborhoods differ with respect to the area available for development, amount of protected open space, and access

to employment. The government provides open space by purchasing land with money raised by property taxes. The model predicts and highlights two important effects of increasing open-space protection within a neighborhood. On the one hand, increasing open space restricts the supply of land available for development, increases the price of the remaining developable land, and increases housing density on that land. Higher land prices and crowding push households away from the neighborhood. On the other hand, protected open space generates a local amenity that makes the neighborhood more attractive thereby pulling households toward the neighborhood. The strength of these push and pull forces and the resulting pattern of development depend on the amenity value of open space. When the amenity value of open space is low, households move away from the neighborhood as open space increases. When the amenity value of the open space is high, increasing open space attracts households and increases housing density and price.

The model provides a theoretical framework for analyzing environmental amenities across space and can be extended to determine the impacts of open-space protection on traffic patterns and congestion and the welfare and distribution of income groups. Equally important, results from the model can alert planners about the possible development impacts of open-space protection in their locales.

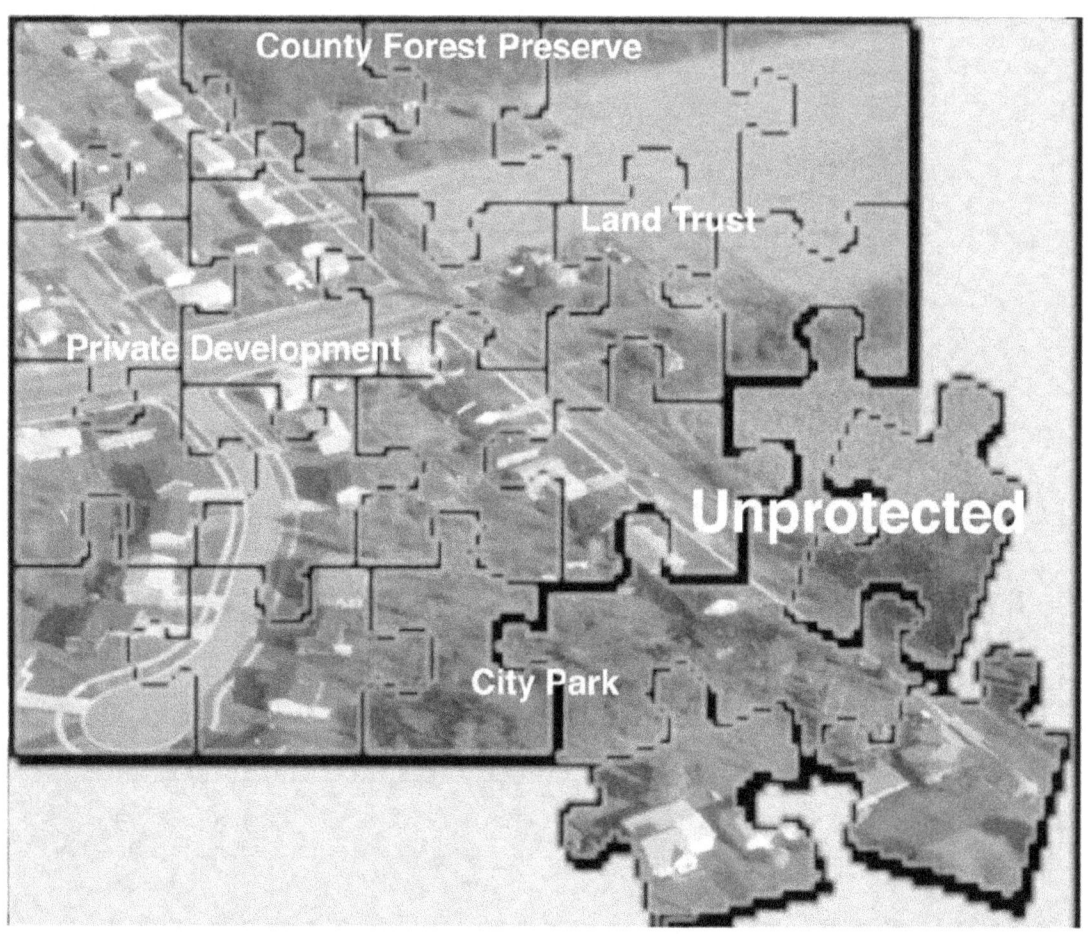

Figure 17.—Open-space protection in a town restricts the supply of land for development and affects land prices and demand for residential development.

Guidelines for Open-Space Neighborhoods on the Urban Fringe

Residential development throughout the Midwest region is expanding into green open spaces on the fringes of metropolitan areas and bringing significant changes to the landscape. **An emerging alternative to haphazard development is the creation of neighborhoods with shared open, natural spaces—the "Open-Space Neighborhood"** (fig. 18). This is one of the options being set forth as part of "smart" residential development.

To understand public perceptions of open-space neighborhoods, social scientists Christine Vogt from Michigan State University and Robert Marans from the University of Michigan, working in cooperation with John Dwyer from the North Central Research Station, interviewed local government officials, developers, environmentalists, and homeowners in Livingston, Washtenaw, and southern Wayne Counties outside of Detroit. From the interviews, the scientists learned that local government officials view open-space neighborhoods favorably because they maintain natural areas and typically provide recreation opportunities for local residents, often reducing the need for new public parks and recreational services. Developers believe such neighborhoods facilitate home sales. Residents feel their quality of life is enhanced. Environmentalists believe such neighborhoods protect natural resources, provide habitat for wildlife, and maintain ecosystems.

The research suggests five major guidelines for policymakers concerning open-space subdivisions. **Connectivity and coordination—** Within each political unit, consider preparing an open-space plan to guide future public and private acquisition and development and establishing mechanisms for linking public and private parcels for ecological, recreational, and esthetic purposes. **Intergovernmental cooperation—**Consider increasing coordination and cooperation between political units in preparing land use plans, developing regulatory systems and approval processes, and managing natural resources. **Natural resource management—**Consider alternative institutional arrangements, approaches, and techniques for managing neighborhood natural resources—to include a range of public-private partnerships. **Equal access to nature and recreational opportunities—**Where open-space neighborhoods exist or are being planned, address issues of access to natural resources and recreation opportunities so the benefits of natural settings can be shared by residents from other parts of the community. **Developer incentives—**Consider incentives to encourage developers to protect and maintain natural resources.

Residential development throughout the Midwest region is expanding into green open spaces on the fringes of metropolitan areas and bringing significant changes to the landscape.

When these policy guidelines are followed, open-space neighborhoods provide a highly effective way of meeting the demands for new housing in developing areas while maintaining natural resources. Such neighborhoods also provide recreational opportunities for local residents while allowing the land to remain on the tax rolls (fig. 19). Finally, these neighborhoods contribute to quality of living in the area and reduce many of the problems associated with more traditional residential developments.

Figure 18.—*A residential development with shared open space.*

Figure 19.—*A residential development with a shared nature trail providing recreation opportunities for local residents.*

Community Identities as Visions for Landscape Change

A community's sense of itself, as felt by its citizens, should play a substantial role in determining visions for landscape change. Landscape planning often emphasizes infrastructure design and development without adequately considering local identities that distinguish one community from another. Community identities are often anchored in tangible environments and events of a community and have the potential to serve as visions for landscape planning.

To investigate the connections between community residents and their environment, social scientist William Stewart of the University of Illinois, with support from the North Central Research Station, interviewed members of rapidly growing communities surrounding Midewin National Tallgrass Prairie just outside the Chicago metropolitan area. Photo-elicitation was used to determine the various meanings that residents attached to local environments. A group of stakeholders were given disposable cameras and asked to photograph places that were important to them (fig. 20). After the film was developed, interviews were conducted and participants were asked to discuss the significance of places they photographed.

Analysis of photographs and interviews focused on understanding the meanings of places that evoked a sense of community. Three types of community-based meanings were represented in the landscape surrounding Midewin. **Places to learn about community landscapes** included various kinds of natural areas, festival sites, and historic transportation routes where people could learn about the functioning of natural ecosystems and the connections between human society and landscapes. **Places to enact community** were gathering places in the community such as churches, local restaurants, murals painted by local artists that represented local heritage, and public parks where people meet and work toward shared goals or demonstrate shared beliefs. **Places to improve community landscapes** included an abandoned mine, eroded farmland stream, and degraded prairie where people have worked together to improve the natural environment. The restoration of Midewin National Tallgrass Prairie is an example of a natural area being a powerful place for individuals to learn about and improve landscapes in ways that facilitate development of various community identities.

Information like that produced in this study helps ensure that positive aspects of existing conditions are maintained and that future landscapes are perceived by constituents as being enhanced.

For planners, identifying shared community identities could form the basis of planning visions that integrate both landscape change and protect valued meanings of local landscapes. In varying degrees, these identities recognize the positive values of landscape change as a restorative and enriching element in building a sense of community. The direction of this research was not to question changes in land use and development, but to provide tools to facilitate changes that enhance a sense of locality and contribute to meaningful senses of community. In the words of Midewin planners: We learned that there is "no need to move back to pre-settlement conditions. Locals do not need the area to be pristine…Evidence of humans is OK." And "The planning process should start with a study like this, that gets stakeholders talking about special places." Information like that produced in this study helps ensure that positive aspects of existing conditions are maintained and that future landscapes are perceived by constituents as being enhanced.

Figure 20.—*Examples of photographs that study participants took to reflect important elements of their community.*

CONCLUSIONS AND NEXT STEPS

This document is a progress report of the Landscape Change Integrated Research Program, highlighting science findings that address the main questions we started out to solve when we first began this venture 5 years ago: (1) How is the landscape changing? (2) What drives landscape change? (3) What are the consequences of landscape change? (4) What do we do about it? Summarizing an ongoing program at a specific point in time is like trying to shoot at a moving target, and in choosing to highlight three to four projects for each question, we necessarily glossed over or left out many other important findings from other projects at various stages of completion (see appendix 2 for a full listing). Drawing on this larger portfolio of work, in this final section we attempt to provide a more generalized synthesis of where we stand in the program and what gaps exist that might be filled in future work.

Patterns

The Changing Midwest landscape assessment has gone far to build a portfolio of human and natural resource information on changes across the Midwest region in recent decades. This county-level information is ideal for giving us the broad picture we need to understand generalized patterns of change across our seven-State region. In addition to the data layers we now have, we should continue to add other human and natural resource information at the county level to our portfolio so we can better address diverse questions and issues facing the region as a whole. Some of

this work is now underway, and soon we will have data layers on such attributes as road density, songbird abundance, and presence of insect defoliators and exotics.

In other cases, however, county data do not yield the level of detail necessary for the analysis of specific questions. Here, we have found major land cover classes derived from satellite imagery at the 1-km^2 resolution and housing density data at the partial block group level provide two key and very versatile building blocks. They allow us not only to look at broad patterns of change across the entire region but also to use these same data to address management questions about particular subareas within a county, metropolitan region, or ecological type. Adding layers at this scale could only be done at great cost and may be unnecessary. Instead, we need to more fully exploit this medium-scale land cover and housing density data to understand the drivers and effects of change.

At the same time, some questions and issues relating to the patterns of change can be understood only by using very fine-grained data such as that obtainable from field study and mapping through GPS and aerial photos. A number of these studies also are underway, including a study of housing development and road networks within selected townships. However, we cannot collect data at this scale across the entire region. Therefore, in the future it will be important to expand these fine-grained studies in a systematic way across important dimensions such as ecological regions so we can derive greater knowledge from them than they are capable of providing as isolated case studies.

Along with these issues of scale, we need to make better use of pattern recognition tools and methods to understand patterns of landscape change. For example, in cooperation with the University of Wisconsin-Madison, we are beginning to use "point-pattern analysis" to help understand whether housing locations exhibit random, regular, or clustered patterns of development over time. Concepts from landscape ecology and spatial analysis tools such as FragStats also will be useful in this respect.

Our analyses of what is driving development-related landscape change in the region point clearly to North Central's amenity resources—especially its forests, lakes, and rivers—as major forces of change.

Finally, we can learn a great deal more about the critical patterns of landscape change by tapping into the expertise of our region's stakeholders. The study of forestland ownership parcelization and development in northern Wisconsin has already been mentioned in this document. Conducting similar listening sessions in other places around the region could prove instrumental in identifying how and where change is taking place. This kind of qualitative, perceptual information is not often available through maps or other published data sources and can thus serve as an early warning system for incipient changes within the region.

Drivers

Our analyses of what is driving development-related landscape change in the region point clearly to North Central's amenity resources—especially its forests, lakes, and rivers—as major forces of change. Although these amenity resources are driving second-home development in the northern and southern portions of the region, our studies indicate related

socioeconomic, demographic, and technological forces are also at work, including greater surplus income among some individuals, an overall aging of the population, and the presence and improvement of roads that provide improved access to rural home sites.

One area where decisionmakers could benefit from a more systematic study of the drivers of change in rural areas would be in the modeling and prediction of outcomes of policy alternatives aimed at protecting resource values and guiding growth. NCRS social scientist Dave Bengston has identified a range of such policies in place regionally and nationally, yet he notes that little has been done to quantify how these policies have worked to achieve their intended purposes. Another driver that could have big effects on the forests of the region is the globalization of industrial forest-land ownership. In States such as Wisconsin, 90 percent of the industrial lands changed hands in the last few years, many of which have gone from locally owned companies with a primary timber emphasis to larger, more diversified corporations. No drastic effects of such changeovers have been reported, yet many of the region's stakeholders are concerned about potential changes over the longer term and the effects they might have on timber supply and other resource concerns.

Some of the same drivers at work in the rural areas of the Midwest region also are playing a role in the landscape change of our region's metropolitan areas. Urban geographers, planners, and others working outside the Station have developed models of metropolitan growth by examining proposed highway extensions, regional economic forecasts, development policies, and other drivers to help assess future urban form over the next few decades. These models often do not place much attention on natural resource protection issues, nor do they look beyond their own metropolitan area of concern to examine potential changes across a multistate region. Within this context, a potential role for the North Central Research Station might be to synthesize the results of these individual urban growth modeling efforts across our seven-State region, to look at common and divergent change drivers and to highlight potential changes to forest and other critical natural resource features.

Effects

Our research to date has just begun to address the effects of landscape change. Of the spectrum of ecosystem-related landscape changes, our scientists have thus far focused on (1) biotic changes—the effects of urbanization on songbird species and abundance and on oak disease and mortality; (2) land resource changes—the effects of forest fragmentation on timber productivity; and (3) atmospheric changes—patterns of ozone transport within and outside the region, with implications for forest health and productivity. Besides topic and content areas, these studies differ along a number of other important dimensions. Some focus on a specific site or area while others cover the entire Midwest region and beyond. Some focus on impacts at the metropolitan fringe while others look at rural and wildland landscapes. And some look at problems unique to the northern ecosystems of the Midwest region while others deal with issues characteristic of the forests and urban areas of the region's central and southern portions.

Because the landscape change program has from the very beginning been organized around understanding the *process of change* more than on any one particular resource,

perhaps it has not been so critical that our initial set of studies was tightly coordinated. Future work, however, could benefit from embedding questions about the landscape change processes within a tighter set of conceptual or geographic boundaries so as to allow for more systematic comparison and analysis.

Two strategies for such future work might prove fruitful. The first approach, suggested in our original charter but not yet acted upon, would be to undertake a place-based approach. Here, we would select three to five prototypical areas within the region where issues of landscape change are critical but different from one another. From these, the effects on the ecosystem could be thoroughly assessed. A second approach would be content oriented, and here we would look to the other two integrated research programs for direction and coordination. As we have seen thus far, forest productivity and riparian landscapes are critical content areas for landscape change. Many stakeholders are concerned about the effects of development on forest health, timber supply, and other forest productivity issues; with lakes and streams being such key amenity attractions for development and use, an obvious priority area should examine development impacts on riparian resources.

Our research to date has just begun to address the effects of landscape change.

Future studies should address not only the ecosystem effects of development-related change, but also those changes that affect people. Although a few program-sponsored studies to date have provided an overview of what these effects might be—restrictions on recreational access to private lands and loss of historic resources, to name two—little systematic or indepth work has yet been accomplished.

39

The importance of providing a balanced view of the effects of changes to people cannot be overemphasized here. Although most work to date has focused on negative impacts, documenting the benefits of development-related growth and change can provide important information to decisionmakers on how future landscape change might be appropriately guided to maximize benefits and minimize impacts.

Future studies should address not only the ecosystem effects of development-related change, but also those changes that affect people.

Strategies

Research to date in our fourth and last problem area has been largely social in nature. Studies here have looked at policies aimed at mitigating the negative effects of landscape change, studied people's responses to alternative housing development designed to conserve open space, and examined how different socially desirable goals result in alternative land acquisition strategies. Most of these have focused on urban and urban fringe areas, and although they may have implications for the broader Midwest region, they have tended to examine particular metropolitan areas in the southern or central portion of the region.

Because many response strategies begin at the policy and planning level, social science approaches seem to be an appropriate focus for this area of the Landscape Change Program. However, field studies and experiments designed to examine factors to protect or rehabilitate sites and landscapes may provide useful information that could also advance research in the Landscape Change Program. For example, stream naturalization strategies developed by

NCRS scientists as part of the ecological rehabilitation of Lake Calumet in southeast Chicago speak directly to the Landscape Change Program goals, as do projects undertaken for the ecological restoration of urban park, rural agricultural, and wildland forest lands throughout the Midwest region. As mentioned above, such work might be conducted within a place-based assessment or within priorities established by the other integrated programs.

Future Directions

This final chapter has identified a number of potential future directions for the Landscape Change Integrated Research and Development Program. Certainly other courses could be taken as well. One fundamental question is whether the program should continue to focus only on development-related landscape change or should expand or shift direction to address other landscape changes such as those from natural disturbances. Such a shift might make sense given the knowledge we might gain from comparing the similarities and differences between different types of disturbances; it also might make sense given new priorities for Forest Service research such as wildland fire and invasive species.

As we move ahead, we will need to continue to rely upon our partners to help us identify and work on research that matters to the constituents of the Midwest region. Please contact us with your questions and ideas so that we can work together to create the knowledge needed to guide the planning and management of our future landscape.

APPENDIX 1: CONTACT AND PUBLICATION INFORMATION FOR RESEARCH HIGHLIGHTS

How is the Landscape Changing?

The Changing Midwest: An Atlas of Landscape Change
Station contacts:

        Eric J. Gustafson

        Robert S. Potts

Web site:

        The Changing Midwest at http://www.ncrs.fs.fed.us/IntegratedPrograms/lc/

Patterns of Housing Density Change Across the Midwest region, 1940-2000
Station contact:

        Susan I. Stewart

Station partners:

        Roger B. Hammer, Department of Rural Sociology, University of Wisconsin-Madison

        Volker C. Radeloff, Department of Forest Ecology and Management, University of Wisconsin-Madison

Publications:

    Hammer, R.B.: Stewart, S.I.; Winkler, R.; *et al.* 2004.

    Characterizing spatial and temporal residential density patterns from 1940-1990 across the North Central United States. Landscape and Urban Planning. 69: 183-189.

    Stewart, S.I.; Radeloff, V.C.; Hammer, R.B. 2003.

    Characteristics and location of the Wildland-Urban Interface in the United States. In: Proceedings, 2d International wildland fire ecology and fire management workshop; 2003 November 16-20; Orlando, FL. 6 p.

    Radeloff, V.C.; Hammer, R.B.; Stewart, S.I. [In review].

    'Sprawl' and forest fragmentation in the U.S. Midwest from 1940 to 2000. Conservation Biology.

Land Cover Change in the Midwest region
Station contacts:

        Eric J. Gustafson

        Robert S. Potts

Station partners:

        Daniel G. Brown and Kathleen M. Bergen, School of Natural Resources and Environment, University of Michigan

Publication:

    Bergen, K.M.; Brown, D.G.; Rutherford, J.; Gustafson, E. 2002.

    Hotspots of land-cover change in the North-Central region using USGS LUDA and NOAA AVHRR. Proceedings, IEEE IGARSS 2002; June 2002; Toronto.

Dynamics of Ozone in the Western Great Lakes Region

Station contact:

> Warren E. Heilman

Station partner:

> Jerome D. Fast, Department of Energy, Battelle Pacific Northwest National Laboratory

Publications:

Fast, J.D.; Heilman, W.E.; Bian, X. 1998.

Weather patterns associated with high ozone concentrations in the Great Lakes region. In: 23d conference on agricultural and forest meteorology; 1998 November 2-6; Albuquerque, NM. Boston, MA: American Meteorological Society: 333-336.

Fast, J.D.; Heilman, W.E. 2002a.

The effect of lake temperatures and emissions on ozone exposure in the western Great Lakes region. Journal of Applied Meteorology. 42(9): 1197-1217.

Fast, J.D.; Heilman, W.E. 2002b.

The effect of lake temperatures on ozone in the western Great Lakes region. In: 25th conference on agricultural and forest meteorology; 2002 May 20-24; Norfolk, VA. Boston, MA: American Meteorological Society: J66-J67.

What Drives Landscape Change?

Amenity Migration as a Driver of Landscape Change

Station contact:

> Susan I. Stewart

Station partner:

> Kenneth M. Johnson, Loyola University, Chicago, IL

Publications:

Johnson, K.M. 2002.

The rural rebound of the 1990s and beyond. In: Levitt, James N., ed. Conservation in the Internet age: threats and opportunities. Washington, DC: Island Press: 63-82.

Stewart, S.I. 2002.

Amenity migration. In: Luft, K.; MacDonald, S., comps. Trends 2000: shaping the future: 5th outdoor recreation & tourism trends symposium; 2000 September 17-20; Lansing, MI. East Lansing, MI: Michigan State University: 369-378.

Accessibility as a Driver of Landscape Change

Station contact:

> Paul H. Gobster

Station partner:

> Mark G. Rickenbach, Department of Forest Ecology and Management, University of Wisconsin-Madison.

Publications:

Rickenbach, M.G.; Gobster, P.H. 2003.
Stakeholders' perceptions of parcelization in Wisconsin's northwoods. Journal of Forestry. 101(6): 18-23.

Gobster, P.H.; Rickenbach, M.G. 2004.
Stakeholder perceptions of private forestland parcelization and development: landscape change in Wisconsin's northwoods. Landscape and Urban Planning. 69: 165-182.

Gobster, P.H.; Schmidt, T.L. 2000.
The use of amenity indicators in anticipating private forestland parcelization: a look at the Lake States' northwoods. In: DeCoster, L.A., ed. Forest fragmentation 2000: a conference on sustaining private forests in the 21st century; 2000 September 17-20; Annapolis, MD. Alexandria, VA: The Sampson Group: 171-180.

Homeowners' and Developers' Views of Nature

Station contact:

Paul H. Gobster

Station partners:

Rachel Kaplan, School of Natural Resources and Environment, University of Michigan
Maureen E. Austin, Environmental Science Department, Alaska Pacific University

Publications:

Kaplan, R.; Austin, M.E. 2004.
Out in the country: sprawl and the quest for nature nearby. Landscape and Urban Planning. 69: 235-243.

Austin, M.E. 2004.
Resident perspectives of the open space conservation subdivision in Hamburg Township, Michigan. Landscape and Urban Planning. 69: 245-253.

Austin, M.E.; Kaplan, R. 2003.
Resident involvement in natural resource management: open space conservation design in practice. Local Environment. 8(2): 141-154.

Kaplan, R.; Austin, M.E.; Kaplan, S. 2004.
Open space communities: resident perception, nature benefits, and terminological problems. Journal of the American Planning Association. 70(3): n.p.

What are the Consequences of Landscape Change?

Effects of Urbanization on Songbird Populations

Station contact:

Frank Thompson

Station partner:

Dirk E. Burhans, Department of Fisheries and Wildlife, University of Missouri-Columbia

Publications:

Thompson, F.R.; Burhans, D.E. 2003.
Predation of songbird nests differs by predator and between field and forest habitats. Journal of Wildlife Management. 67(2): 408-416.

Thompson, F.R.; Burhans, D.E.; Root, B. 2002.
Effects of point count protocol on bird abundance and variability estimates and power to detect population trends. Journal of Field Ornithology. 73(2): 141-150.

Pagen, R.W.; Thompson, F.R.; Burhans, D.E. 2001.
A comparison of point-count and mist-net detections of songbirds by habitat and time-of-season. Journal of Field Ornithology. 73(1): 53-59.

Burhans, D.E.; Dearborn, D.; Thompson, F.R.; Faaborg, J. 2002.
Factors affecting predation at songbird nests in old fields. Journal of Wildlife Management. 66(1): 240-249.

Effects of Housing Density on Timber Harvesting

Station contact:
Susan I. Stewart

Station partners:
Volker C. Radeloff and Alexia A. Sabor, Department of Forest Ecology and Management, University of Wisconsin-Madison
Roger B. Hammer, Department of Rural Sociology, University of Wisconsin-Madison

Publication:
Sabor, A.A.; Radeloff, V.C.; Hammer, R.B.; Stewart, S.I. 2003.
Relationships between housing density and timber harvest in the Upper Lake States. In: Buse, L.J.; Perera, A.H., comps. Meeting emerging ecological, economic, and social challenges in the Great Lakes region: popular summaries. For. Res. Inf. Pap. 155. Sault Ste. Marie, ON: Ontario Ministry of Natural Resources, Ontario Forest Research Institute: 80-82.

Protecting the Health of Oak Forests in Urbanizing Landscapes

Station contact:
Jennifer Juzwik

Station partners:
Frank Pfleger, Department of Plant Pathology, University of Minnesota, St. Paul
Brian Loeffelholz, Gary Johnson, and Marvin Bauer, Department of Forest Resources, University of Minnesota, St. Paul
Linda Haugen, USDA Forest Service, Northeastern Area State and Private Forestry, St. Paul, MN
Steve Cook, Cook Company, West St. Paul, MN
Joan Elwell, JD Grafix, New Brighton, MN

Publication:
Juzwik, J.; Cook, S.; Haugen, L.; Elwell, J. 2003.
Oak wilt: people and trees, a community approach to management. Gen. Tech. Rep. NC-240. St. Paul, MN: U.S. Department of Agriculture, Forest Service, North Central Research Station. CD-ROM version 2004 v 1.3.

The Perceived Impacts of Urban Sprawl Across Thirteen Midwestern Cities

Station contact:

David N. Bengston

Station partners:

David P. Fan, Department of Genetics and Cell Biology, University of Minnesota

Edward Goetz, Humphrey Institute of Public Affairs, University of Minnesota

Publication:

Bengston, D.N.; Fan, D.P.; Potts, R.S.; Goetz, E.G. [In review].

Monitoring the social environment for planning: a computer content analysis approach. Journal of the American Planning Association.

What Do We Do About Landscape Change?

Public Policies for Managing Urban Growth and Protecting Open Space

Station contact:

David N. Bengston

Station partners:

Kristen C. Nelson, Department of Forest Resources, University of Minnesota

Jenna Fletcher, Minnesota Forest Resources Council

Publication:

Bengston, D.N.; Fletcher, J.; Nelson, K.C. 2004.

Public policies for managing urban growth and protecting open space: policy instruments and lessons learned in the United States. Landscape and Urban Planning. 69: 271-286.

Goal Tradeoffs in Metropolitan Open-Space Protection

Station contact:

Robert G. Haight

Station partner:

Frances R. Homans, Department of Applied Economics, University of Minnesota

Publications:

Ruliffson, J.A.; Gobster, P.H.; Haight, R.G.; Homans, F.R. 2002.

Niches in the urban forest: organizations and their role in acquiring metropolitan open space. Journal of Forestry. 100(6): 16-23.

Ruliffson, J.A.; Haight, R.G.; Gobster, P.H.; Homans, F.R. 2003.

Metropolitan natural area protection to maximize public access and species representation. Environmental Science and Policy. 6: 291-299.

Impacts of Open-Space Protection on Development Pattern

Station contact:

Robert G. Haight

Station partner:

Stephen Polasky, Department of Applied Economics, University of Minnesota

Publication:

Tajibaeva, L.; Haight, R.G.; Polasky, S. [In review].

A discrete space urban model with environmental amenities. Journal of Environmental Economics and Management.

Guidelines for Open-Space Neighborhoods on the Urban Fringe

Station contact:

Paul H. Gobster

Station partners:

Christine A. Vogt, Department of Park, Recreation and Tourism Resources, Michigan State University

Robert W. Marans, College of Architecture and Urban Planning, University of Michigan.

Publications:

Vogt, Christine A.; Marans, Robert W. 2002.

Understanding landscape change in open space neighborhoods: views from developers and residents. In: Schuster, Rudy, comp., ed. Proceedings, 2002 Northeastern recreation research symposium; 2002 April 13-16; Bolton Landing, NY. Gen. Tech. Rep. NE-302. Newtown Square, PA: U.S. Department of Agriculture, Forest Service, Northeastern Research Station: 72-78.

Vogt, C.A.; Marans, R.W. [In review].

Open-space neighborhoods: resident views on emerging residential developments. Journal of Park and Recreation Administration.

Marans, Robert W. 2003.

Understanding environmental quality through quality of life studies: the 2001 DAS and its use of subjective and objective indicators. Landscape and Urban Planning. 65: 73-83.

Vogt, Christine A.; Marans, Robert W. 2001.

The role, use and benefits of natural recreation areas within and near residential subdivisions. In: Todd, Sharon, ed. Proceedings, 2001 Northeastern recreation research symposium; 2001 April 1-3; Bolton Landing, NY. Gen. Tech. Rep. NE-289. Newtown Square, PA: U.S. Department of Agriculture, Forest Service, Northeastern Research Station: 208-213.

Community Identities as Visions for Landscape Change

Station contact:

Lynne M. Westphal

Station partner:

William P. Stewart, Department of Leisure Studies, University of Illinois

Publication:

Stewart, W.P.; Liebert, D.; Larkin, K.W. 2004.

Community identities as visions for landscape change. Landscape and Urban Planning. 69: 315-334.

APPENDIX 2: NCRS-SPONSORED LANDSCAPE CHANGE RESEARCH, 1999-2003

Table 1.—List of landscape change studies sponsored by NCRS

Year initiated	Study title	NC contact(s)	NC contact info	Cooperator(s)	Cooperator contact info
1997	Landscape change along ecological and cultural gradients in the Lower St. Croix River Valley	Eric Gustafson, NC-4153, Rhinelander	egustafson@fs.fed.us (715-362-1152)	Evelyn Howell, Dept. Landscape Archit., Univ. of Wisconsin-Madison	
1998	Simulating the effects of forest management and natural disturbances on landscape patterns of the Northwestern Wisconsin Pine Barrens	Eric Gustafson, NC-4153, Rhinelander	egustafson@fs.fed.us (715-362-1152)	David Mladenoff and Volker Radeloff, Dept. For. Ecol. and Manage., Univ. of Wisconsin-Madison	
1999	Recreation-amenity migration in urban proximate areas	Susan Stewart, NC-4902, Evanston	sistewart@fs.fed.us (847-866-9311 x13)	Kenneth Johnson, Dept. of Socio., Loyola Univ., Chicago	kjohnso@luc.edu (773-508-3461)
1999	Understanding the dynamics of residential choice: the role of the natural environment	John Dwyer, NC-4902, Evanston	jdwyer@fs.fed.us (847-866-9311 x17)	Robert Marans, Coll. Archit. and Urban Plann., Univ. of Michigan, Christine Vogt, Dept. Park, Recreation and Tourism Resour., Michigan State Univ.	marans@umich.edu (734-763-4583), vogtc@pilot.msu.edu (517-353-5190 x128)
1999	Landscape change at Midewin Prairie	Lynne Westphal, NC-4902, Evanston	lwestphal@fs.fed.us (847-866-9311 x11)	William Stewart, Dept. Leisure Studies, Univ. of Illinois at Urbana-Champaign	wstewart@uiuc.edu (217-244-4532)
1999	Nature at the urban edge: ecological-psychological values	Lynne Westphal, NC-4902, Evanston	lwestphal@fs.fed.us (847-866-9311 x11)	Rachel Kaplan, School of Nat. Resour. and Environ., Univ. of Michigan	rkaplan@snre.umich.edu (734-763-1061)
1999	The role of urban forests and green-frastructure on suburban sprawl and on housing choice decisions: an explora-tory study	Herbert Schroeder, NC-4902, Evanston	hschroeder@fs.fed.us (847-866-9311 x15)	Rohit Verma, David Eccles, School of Business, Univ. of Utah	rohit.verma@business.utah.edu (801-585-5263)
1999	Perceptions of development, sustainability, and nature: a narrative study of real estate developers	Paul Gobster, NC-4902, Evanston	pgobster@fs.fed.us (847-866-9311 x16)	Karen Vigmostad, Dept. Resour. Dev., Michigan State Univ.	kvigmostad@nemw.org (202-544-5200)
1999	Exploring goal tradeoffs in metropolitan natural area protection	Paul Gobster, NC-4902, Evanston; and Robert Haight, NC-4803, St. Paul	pgobster@fs.fed.us (847-866-9311 x16); rhaight@fs.fed.us (651-649-5178)	Frances Homans, Dept. Appl. Econ., Univ. of Minnesota	fhomans@dept.agecon.umn.edu (612-625-6220)

(Table 1 continued on next page)

(Table 1 continued)

Year	Study title	NC contact(s)	NC contact info	Cooperator(s)	Cooperator contact info
1999	Simulating forest landscape change in Indiana	Frank Thompson, NC-4154, Columbia	frthompson@fs.fed.us (573-875-5341)	David Larsen, Univ. of Missouri	
1999	Predicting scenic perception in a changing landscape	Paul Gobster, NC-4902, Evanston	pgobster@fs.fed.us (847-866-9311 x16)	James Palmer, Dept. Landscape Archit., State Univ. of New York-Syracuse	zooey@mailbox. syr.edu (315-470-6548)
1999	Landscape change in the Upper Midwest	Thomas Crow, NC-4101, Grand Rapids; and Sue Lietz, NC-4153, Rhinelander	tcrow@fs.fed.us (218-326-7110), slietz@fs.fed.us (715-362-1142)	Barbara Andersen, Dept. Landscape Archit., Univ. of Idaho	bjander@uidaho. edu (208-885-9821)
1999	Causes of land-scape pattern	Thomas Crow, NC-4101, Grand Rapids	tcrow@fs.fed.us (218-326-7110)	George Host, Nat. Resour. Res. Inst., Univ. of Minnesota-Duluth, David Mladenoff, Dept. For. Ecol. and Manage., Univ. of Wisconsin-Madison	ghost@umn.edu (218-720-4264), djmladen@facstaff. wisc.edu (608-262-1992)
2000	Characterizing historical and modern disturbance regimes in the Lake States	David Cleland, NC-4153, Rhinelander	dcleland@fs.fed.us (715-362-1117)	Donald Dickmann, Michigan State Univ.	
2000	Conservation priorities for lowland forest birds on the St. Croix River	John Probst, NC-4153, Rhinelander	jprobst@fs.fed.us (715-362-1156)	Mike Worland and Francesca Cuthbert, Dept. Fish. and Wildl., Univ. of Minnesota	worl0014@umn.edu (715-282-4925), cuthb001@umn.edu (612-624-1756)
2000	Landscape level analysis linking urban sprawl and aquatic ecosystems	John Dwyer, NC-4902, Evanston	jdwyer@fs.fed.us (847-866-9311 x17)	Daniel Brown, School of Nat. Resour. and Environ., Univ. of Michigan	danbrown@umich.edu (734-963-2195)
2000	Aligning social and ecological drivers of urban landscape change: the Calumet Urban Riparian Area	Lynne Westphal, NC-4902, Evanston	lwestphal@fs.fed.us (847-866-9311 x11)	Joan Nassauer, School of Nat. Resour. and Environ., Univ. of Michigan	nassauer@umich. edu (734-763-9893)
2000	Policies for managing forest landscape change: an assessment and an agenda for future research	David Bengston, NC-4803, St. Paul	dbengston@fs.fed.us (651-649-5162)	Kristen Nelson, Dept. For. Resour., Univ. of Minnesota	kcn@umn.edu (612-624-1277)
2000	Demographic change and landscape management in the Midwest region: a focus on wildlife resources	John Dwyer, NC-4902, Evanston	jdwyer@fs.fed.us (847-866-9311 x17)	Alan Marsinko Dept. For. Resour., Clemson Univ.	AMMRS@clemson. edu (864-656-4839)
2000	Ethnography of a growth coalition	Paul Gobster, NC-4902, Evanston	pgobster@fs.fed.us (847-866-9311 x16)	Karen Vigmostad Dept. Resour. Dev. Michigan State Univ.	kvigmostad@ nemw.org (202-544-5200)

(Table 1 continued on next page)

(Table 1 continued)

Year	Study title	NC contact(s)	NC contact info	Cooperator(s)	Cooperator contact info
2000	Midwestern landscapes in transition: identification of past and future residential development and demographic change hotspots across the Midwest region	Susan Stewart, NC-4902, Evanston	sistewart@fs.fed.us (847-866-9311 x13)	Paul Voss and Roger Hammer, Dept. Rural Sociol., and Volker Radeloff and Donald Field, Dept. For. Ecol. and Manage., Univ. of Wisconsin	voss@ssc.wisc.edu (608-262-9526), rhammer@facstaff. wisc.edu (608-263-2898), radeloff@facstaff. wisc.edu (608-265-6321) drfield@facstaff. wisc.edu (608-263-0853),
2000	Extending research on the dynamics of residential choice: the appeal of older neighborhoods	Susan Stewart, NC-4902, Evanston	sistewart@fs.fed.us (847-866-9311 x13)	Robert Marans, Coll. Archit. and Urban Plann., Univ. of Michigan, Christine Vogt, Dept. Park, Recreation and Tourism Resour., Michigan State Univ.	marans@umich.edu (734-763-4583), vogtc@pilot.msu.edu (517-353-5190 x128)
2000	Social costs and benefits of forest buffers at the urban fringe	Paul Gobster, NC-4902, Evanston	pgobster@fs.fed.us (847-866-9311 x16)	William Sullivan, Human-Environ. Res. Lab., Univ. of Illinois at Urbana-Champaign	wcsulliv@uiuc.edu (217-244-5156)
2000	Meaning, community, and landscape change in Calumet	Lynne Westphal, NC-4902, Evanston	lwestphal@fs.fed.us (847-866-9311 x11)	Daniel Cook, Dept. Advertising, Univ. of Illinois at Urbana-Champaign	dtcook@uiuc.edu (217-333-1602)
2000	Environmental factors influencing recreation choice in post-industrial landscapes	Lynne Westphal, NC-4902, Evanston	lwestphal@fs.fed.us (847-866-9311 x11)	David Klenosky, Dept. Health and Kinesiology, Purdue Univ.	klenosky@purdue.edu (765-494-0865)
2000	Urban sprawl and a sense of self-in-place: a thematic analysis of compact and metropolitan urban perceptions	Herbert Schroeder, NC-4902, Evanston	hschroeder@fs.fed.us (847-866-9311 x15)	James Cantrill, Communications and Performance Studies, Northern Michigan Univ.	jcantril@nmu.edu (906-227-2061)
2000	Conflict in interface forestry: nature, science, landscape change, and forest productivity	John Dwyer, NC-4902, Evanston	jdwyer@fs.fed.us (847-866-9311 x17)	Bruce Hull, Dept. of For. Resour., Virginia Tech	hullrb@vt.edu (540-231-7272)
2000	Midwestern landscapes in transition: demographic characteristics and population and housing unit projections in the Midwest region	Susan Stewart, NC-4902, Evanston	sistewart@fs.fed.us (847-866-9311 x13)	Paul Voss and Roger Hammer, Dept. Rural Sociol., and Volker Radeloff and Donald Field, Dept. For. Ecol. and Manage., Univ. of Wisconsin-Madison	voss@ssc.wisc.edu (608-262-9526), rhammer@facstaff. wisc.edu (608-263-2898), radeloff@facstaff. wisc.edu (608-265-6321), drfield@facstaff. wisc.edu (608-263-0853)

(Table 1 continued on next page)

(Table 1 continued)

Year	Study title	NC contact(s)	NC contact info	Cooperator(s)	Cooperator contact info
2000	People and the landscape: county-level net migration in the U.S., 1990 to 2000 with analysis of age-specific migration selectivity to recreational and high amenity counties	Susan Stewart, NC-4902, Evanston	sistewart@fs.fed.us (847-866-9311 x13)	Paul Voss, Roger Hammer, and Glen Fuguitt, Dept. Rural Sociol., Univ. of Wisconsin-Madison	voss@ssc.wisc.edu (608-262-9526), rhammer@facstaff. wisc.edu (608-263-2898), fuguitt@ssc. wisc.edu (608-263-2899)
2000	Nest predation and nest predators of songbirds along an urban-rural gradient	Frank Thompson, NC-4154, Columbia	frthompson@fs.fed.us (573-875-5341)	Dirk Burhans, Dept. Fish. and Wildl., Univ. of Missouri	burhansd@missouri. edu (573-875-5341)
2000	Historical impact of urbanization on oak forest health in the Minneapolis – St. Paul, MN, metro region	Jennifer Juzwik, Kathy Ward, and Paul Castillo, NC-4502, St. Paul	jjuzwik@fs.fed.us (651-649-5114), kward01@fs.fed.us (651-649-5100), pcastillo01@fs.fed.us (651-649-5115)	Kathryn Kromroy, Dept. Plant Path., and Francis Pfleger, Dept. Contin. Edu., Univ. of Minnesota	krom0001@umn.edu (651-292-9222), pfleg001@umn.edu (612-625-4705)
2000	Predicting impacts of development on oaks in Minnesota peri-urban forests	Jennifer Juzwik, NC-4502, St. Paul	jjuzwik@fs.fed.us (651-649-5114)	Gary Johnson, Alan Ek, Paul Bolstad, and Marv Bauer, Dept. For. Resour., Univ. of Minnesota	gjohnson@forestry. umn.edu (612-625-3765), aek@umn.edu (612-624-3400), pbolstad@umn.edu (612-624-9711), mbauer@umn.edu (612-624-3703)
2000	Use of amenity indicators to understand private landownership fragmentation in the Northwoods	Paul Gobster, NC-4902, Evanston; and Thomas Schmidt, NC, St. Paul	pgobster@fs.fed.us (847-866-9311 x16), tschmidt@fs.fed.us (651-649-5131)		
2000	Predicting oak wilt occurrence in urban areas: geo-statistical modeling of the disease in the Minneapolis-St. Paul region	Jennifer Juzwik, Paul Castillo, and Kathy Ward, NC-4502, St. Paul	jjuzwik@fs.fed.us (651-649-5114), pcastillo01@fs.fed.us (651-649-5115), kward01@fs.fed.us (651-649-5100)		
2000	Evaluation of spatial models to predict vulnerability of forest birds to brood parasitism by brown-headed cowbirds	Eric Gustafson, NC-4153, Rhinelander	egustafson@fs.fed.us (715-362-1152)	Gerald Niemi, Nat. Resour. Res. Inst., Univ. of Minnesota-Duluth; Melinda Knutson, USGS, LaCrosse, WI; Mary Hammer Fridberg, Superior National Forest	gniemi@umn.edu (218-720-4270)
2000	Landscape change in the Upper Wabash watershed	Charles Michler, NC-4157, West Lafayette	cmichler@fs.fed.us (765-496-6016)	Purdue Univ.	
2000	Sustaining natural resources on private land in the Central Hardwood Region	Charles Michler, NC-4157, West Lafayette	cmichler@fs.fed.us (765-496-6016)	Purdue Univ., Univ. of Tennessee, Univ. of Missouri	
2000	Factors affecting bird communities in forested riparian corridors in the Midwestern US	Frank Thompson, NC-4154, Columbia	frthompson@fs.fed.us (573-875-5341)	Rebecca Peak, Dept. Fish. and Wildl., Univ. of Missouri	

(Table 1 continued on next page)

(Table 1 continued)

Year	Study title	NC contact(s)	NC contact info	Cooperator(s)	Cooperator contact info
2000	Conservation of disturbance-dependent birds	Frank Thompson, NC-4154 Columbia	frthompson@fs.fed.us (573-875-5341)	Scott Robinson, Dept. Animal Biol., Univ. of Illinois at Urbana-Champaign, Richard DeGraaf, NE-4251, Amherst, MA	skrobins@uiuc.edu (217-333-6857), rdegraaf@fs.fed.us (413-545-0357)
2001	Land cover change in the Midwest region	Robert Potts and Eric Gustafson, NC-4153, Rhinelander	robertpotts@fs.fed.us (715-362-1113), egustafson@fs.fed.us (715-362-1152)	Daniel Brown and Kathleen Bergen, School of Nat. Resour. and Environ., Univ. of Michigan	danbrown@ umich.edu (734-963-2195), kbergen@umich.edu (734-615-8834)
2001	Socioeconomic foundations for ozone modeling	Pam Jakes, NC-4803, St. Paul; and Susan Stewart, NC-4902, Evanston	pjakes@fs.fed.us (651-649-5163), sistewart@fs.fed.us (847-866-9311 x13)	Roger Hammer, Dept. Rural Sociol., Univ. of Wisconsin-Madison	rhammer@facstaff. wisc.edu (608-263-2898)
2001	Linking NCRS hotspots analysis and the Northern Global Climate Change Program	Susan Stewart, NC-4902, Evanston	sistewart@fs.fed.us (847-866-9311 x13)	Volker Radeloff, Dept. For. Ecol. and Manage., Univ. of Wisconsin-Madison	radeloff@facstaff. wisc.edu (608-265-6321)
2001	Demographic trends in national forest, recreational, retirement, and amenity areas of the United States	Susan Stewart, NC-4902, Evanston	sistewart@fs.fed.us (847-866-9311 x13)	Kenneth Johnson, Dept. Sociol., Loyola Univ., Chicago	kjohnso@luc.edu (773-508-3461)
2001	Effects of housing change on forest productivity in the Lake States	Susan Stewart, NC-4902, Evanston	sistewart@fs.fed.us (847-866-9311 x13)	Volker Radeloff, Dept. of For. Ecol. and Manage., Univ. of Wisconsin	radeloff@facstaff. wisc.edu (608-265-6321)
2001	Habitat fragmentation due to housing change in the Northwoods: spatial pattern of housing units through time	Susan Stewart, NC-4902, Evanston	sistewart@fs.fed.us (847-866-9311 x13)	Volker Radeloff, Dept. For. Ecol. and Manage., Univ. of Wisconsin-Madison	radeloff@facstaff. wisc.edu (608-265-6321)
2001	Landscape-level habitat suitability models for 12 species in southern Missouri	William Dijak and Frank Thompson, NC-4154, Columbia	wdijak@fs.fed.us (573-875-5341 x241), frthompson@fs.fed. us (573-875-5341)	Michael Andrew Larson and Joshua Millspaugh, Dept. Fish. and Wildl., Univ. of Missouri	LarsonM@missouri.edu (573-882-9424), MillspaughJ@ missouri.edu (573-882-9423)
2001	Social implications of landscape change: an analysis of survey data covering SE Michigan	Paul Gobster, NC-4902, Evanston	pgobster@fs.fed.us (847-866-9311 x16)	Robert Marans, Coll. Archit. and Urban Plann., Univ. of Michigan, Christine Vogt, Dept. Park, Recreation and Tourism Resour., Michigan State Univ.	marans@umich.edu (734-763-4583), vogtc@pilot. msu.edu (517-353-5190 x128)
2001	Natural resources and decisionmaking for local planning	Lynne Westphal, NC-4902, Evanston	lwestphal@fs.fed.us (847-866-9311 x11)	Rachel Kaplan, School of Nat. Resour. and Environ., Univ. of Michigan	rkaplan@snre. umich.edu (734-763-1061)
2001	Open space and property values: an urban economics model with application to the Twin Cities Region	Robert Haight, NC-4803, St. Paul	rhaight@fs.fed.us (651-649-5178)	Steve Polasky, Dept. Appl. Econ., Univ. of Minnesota	polas004@umn.edu (612-625-9213)

51

(Table 1 continued on next page)

(*Table 1 continued*)

Year	Study title	NC contact(s)	NC contact info	Cooperator(s)	Cooperator contact info
2001	Landscape change in southern Wisconsin: residential preferences and subdivision development beyond the urban fringe	Paul Gobster, NC-4902, Evanston	pgobster@fs.fed.us (847-866-9311 x16)	James LaGro, Jr., Dept. Urban and Reg. Plann., Univ. of Wisconsin-Madison, and Barbara Andersen, Dept. Landscape Archit., Univ. of Idaho	jalagro@facstaff. wisc.edu (608-263-6507), bjander@uidaho.edu (208-885-9821)
2001	Predicting ecological and social impacts of riparian landuse in a North Central landscape	Pam Jakes, NC-4803, St. Paul	pjakes@fs.fed.us (651-649-5163)	Kristen Nelson, Dept. For. Resour., Univ. of Minnesota	kcn@umn.edu (612-624-1277)
2001	3-D visualization of landscape change under land management and fire effects	Eric Gustafson, NC-4153, Rhinelander	egustafson@fs.fed.us (715-362-1152)	Bo Song, Dept. For. Resour., Clemson Univ.	bosong@clemson.edu (843-545-5673)
2001	Investigating factors limiting dispersal success by Waabizheshi (American marten) in Wisconsin	Patrick Zollner, NC-4153, Rhinelander	pzollner@fs.fed.us (715-362-1150)	Jonathan Gilbert, Great Lakes Indian Wildl. and Fish. Comm.	jgilbert@glifwc.org (715-682-6619 x121)
2001	Simulation of alternative landscape change scenarios for the Boundary Waters Canoe Area	Thomas Crow, NC-4101, Grand Rapids	tcrow@fs.fed.us (218-326-7110)	Dave Mladenoff, Dept. For. Ecol. and Manage., Univ. of Wisconsin-Madison	
2001	Forest ownership fragmen-tation in northern Wisconsin: perceptions of stakeholder groups	Paul Gobster, NC-4902, Evanston	pgobster@fs.fed.us (847-866-9311 x16)	Mark Rickenbach, Dept. For. Ecol. and Manage., Univ. of Wisconsin-Madison	mgrickenbach@ facstaff.wisc.edu (608-262-0134)
2001	Where are the hotspots of landscape change in the Midwest region?	Robert Potts and Eric Gustafson, NC-4153, Rhinelander	robertpotts@fs.fed.us (715-362-1113), egustafson@fs.fed.us (715-362-1152)		
2002	Racial, demographic, and age structure shifts in urban, suburban, and rural areas of the Midwest region: implications for recreational and forest usage	Susan Stewart, NC-4902, Evanston	sistewart@fs.fed.us (847-866-9311 x13)	Kenneth Johnson, Dept. Sociol., Loyola Univ., Chicago	kjohnso@luc.edu (773-508-3461)
2002	Land-use decisions on private lands	Susan Stewart, NC-4902, Evanston	sistewart@fs.fed.us (847-866-9311 x13)	Shorna Broussard, Dept. For. and Nat. Resour., Purdue Univ.	srb@fnr.purdue.edu (765-494-3603)
2002	Modeling the relationship between regional land-scape change and tropo-spheric ozone formation	Stephanie Snyder, NC-4803, St. Paul	stephaniesnyder@ fs.fed.us (651-649-5294)	Brian Stone, Univ. of Wisconsin-Madison	
2002	Housing density and the Wildland-Urban Interface across the US	Susan Stewart, NC-4902, Evanston	sistewart@fs.fed.us (847-866-9311 x13)	Volker Radeloff, Dept. For. Ecol. and Manage., Univ. of Wisconsin-Madison	radeloff@facstaff. wisc.edu (608-265-6321)
2002	Land cover and the Wildland-Urban Interface across the US	Susan Stewart, NC-4902, Evanston	sistewart@fs.fed.us (847-866-9311 x13)	Volker Radeloff, Dept. For. Ecol. and Manage., Univ. of Wisconsin-Madison	radeloff@facstaff. wisc.edu (608-265-6321)

(*Table 1 continued on next page*)

(Table 1 continued)

Year	Study title	NC contact(s)	NC contact info	Cooperator(s)	Cooperator contact info
2002	Making metropolitan areas more livable: recognizing and enhancing underappreciated natural resources	Lynne Westphal, NC-4902, Evanston	lwestphal@fs.fed.us (847-866-9311 x11)	Rachel Kaplan, School of Nat. Resour. and Environ., Univ. of Michigan	rkaplan@snre.umich. edu (734-763-1061)
2002	Developing GIS simulation for integrating landscape ecological knowledge into landscape designs	Susan Stewart, NC-4902, Evanston	sistewart@fs.fed.us (847-866-9311 x13)	Daniel Brown, School of Nat. Resour. and Environ., Univ. of Michigan	danbrown@umich.edu (734-963-2195)
2002	Identifying key linkages between water quality and land development patterns in riparian areas in the Midwest region	Stephanie Snyder, NC-4803, St. Paul	stephaniesnyder@ fs.fed.us (651-649-5294)	Larry Baker and Mary Renwick, Univ. of Minnesota	
2002	Tropospheric ozone dynamics in the Western Great Lakes Region— developing ozone precursor emission projections based on future land-use patterns	Warren Heilman, NC-4401, East Lansing	wheilman@fs.fed.us (517-355-7740 x27)	Dept. Energy- Battelle Pacific Northwest Natl. Lab.	
2002	Integrating social values in landscape change assessments	Paul Gobster, NC-4902, Evanston	pgobster@fs.fed.us (847-866-9311 x16)	Mimi Wagner, Dept. Landscape Archit., Iowa State Univ.	mimiw@iastate.edu (515-294-8954)
2002	Guides for management of public lands on the wildland-urban interface	John Dwyer, NC-4902, Evanston	jdwyer@fs.fed.us (847-866-9311 x17)	Deborah Chavez, PSW-4902, Riverside	dchavez@fs.fed.us (909-680-1558)
2002	The changing Midwest: density of population, housing, and seasonal housing	Robert Potts, NC-4153, Rhinelander	robertpotts@fs.fed.us (715-362-1113)	Roger Hammer, Dept. Rural Sociol., Univ. of Wisconsin-Madison	rhammer@facstaff. wisc.edu (608-263-2898)
2002	Why special places are important to people	Herbert Schroeder, NC-4902, Evanston	hschroeder@fs.fed.us (847-866-9311 x15)		
2002	The changing Midwest: personal income from wood products, recreation, and real estate	Robert Potts, NC-4153, Rhinelander	robertpotts@fs.fed.us (715-362-1113)		
2002	Managing the risk of fire on human and ecological communities in the Wildland-Urban Interface	Brian Sturtevant, NC-4153, Rhinelander	bsturtevant@fs.fed.us (715-362-1105)		
2002	Monitoring hotspots of concern about sprawl	David Bengston, NC-4803, St. Paul; and Robert Potts, NC-4153, Rhinelander	dbengston@fs.fed.us (651-649-5162), robertpotts@fs.fed.us (715-362-1113)	David Fan, InfoTrend, St. Paul, MN	fanxx002@umn.edu (612-624-4718)
2002	Is landscape change driving declines in breeding bird populations in the Midwest region?	Frank Thompson, NC-4154, Columbia; and Robert Potts, NC-4153, Rhinelander	frthompson@fs.fed.us (573-875-5341), robertpotts@fs.fed.us (715-362-1113)		
2002	Impacts of landscape pattern on genetic diversity and evolutionary processes	William Mattson, NC-4152, Rhinelander; and Eric Gustafson, NC-4153, Rhinelander	wmattson@fs.fed.us (715-362-1174), egustafson@fs.fed.us (715-362-1152)		

(Table 1 continued on next page)

(Table 1 continued)

Year	Study title	NC contact(s)	NC contact info	Cooperator(s)	Cooperator contact info
2003	Unearthing the benefits of brownfield to green space projects: a study of user and community perceptions and reactions	Lynne Westphal, NC-4902, Evanston	lwestphal@fs.fed.us (847-866-9311 x11)	Christopher DeSousa, Dept. Geogr., Univ. of Wisconsin-Milwaukee	desousa@uwm.edu
2003	Making sense of landscape change: community narratives that facilitate planning	Lynne Westphal, NC-4902, Evanston	lwestphal@fs.fed.us (847-866-9311 x11)	William Stewart, Dept. Leisure Studies, Univ. of Illinois at Urbana-Champaign	wstewart@uiuc.edu (217-244-4532),
2003	Comparing perceptions of riparian function to assessed values and conditions: management in a changing landscape	Paul Gobster, NC-4902, Evanston	pgobster@fs.fed.us (847-866-9311 x16)	Mimi Wagner, Dept. Landscape Archit., Iowa State Univ.	mimiw@iastate.edu (515-294-8954)
2003	Metropolitan trout streams: urban residents' perceptions and management of unique urban resources	David Bengston, NC-4803, St. Paul; and Robert Potts, NC-4153, Rhinelander	dbengston@fs.fed.us (651-649-5162), robertpotts@fs.fed.us (715-362-1113)	Kristen Nelson, Dept. For. Resour., Univ. of Minnesota	kcn@umn.edu (612-624-1277)
2003	Restoring native diversity in agricultural landscapes	Thomas Crow, NC-4101, Grand Rapids	tcrow@fs.fed.us (218-326-7110)	Heidi Asbjornsen, Dept. Nat. Resour., Ecol., and Manage., Iowa State Univ.	hasbjorn@iastate.edu (515-294-7703)
2003	Developing a collaborative modeling approach to assess biological and economic effects of land use decisions	Lynne Westphal, NC-4902, Evanston	lwestphal@fs.fed.us (847-866-9311 x11)	Steve Polasky, Dept. Appl. Econ., Univ. of Minnesota	polas004@umn.edu (612-625-9213)
2003	Mapping the 1990 WUI and 1990-2000 WUI change at the Census Block Level across the United States	Susan Stewart, NC-4902, Evanston	sistewart@fs.fed.us (847-866-9311 x13)	Volker Radeloff, Dept. For. Ecol. and Manage., Univ. of Wisconsin-Madison	radeloff@facstaff. wisc.edu (608-265-6321)
2003	Social characteristics of WUI communities in 1990 and 2000 across the United States	Susan Stewart, NC-4902, Evanston	sistewart@fs.fed.us (847-866-9311 x13)	Roger Hammer, Dept. Rural Sociol., Univ. of Wisconsin	rhammer@facstaff. wisc.edu (608-263-2898)
2003	Analyzing temporal and spatial dynamics of the WUI from 1940-2030 in the Western U.S.	Susan Stewart, NC-4902, Evanston	sistewart@fs.fed.us (847-866-9311 x13)	Volker Radeloff, Dept. For. Ecol. and Manage., Univ. of Wisconsin-Madison	radeloff@facstaff. wisc.edu (608-265-6321)
2003	Valuing rural forest land: a property price approach	Stephanie Snyder, NC-4803, St. Paul; and Susan Stewart, NC-4902, Evanston	stephaniesnyder@ fs.fed.us (651-649-5294), sistewart@fs.fed.us (847-866-9311 x13)	Mike Kilgore, Dept. For. Resour., Univ. of Minnesota	mkilgore@umn.edu (612-624-6298)
2003	From the logger's perspective: land tenure and timber supply in Wisconsin, Michigan's Upper Peninsula, and Indiana	Paul Gobster, NC-4902, Evanston	pgobster@fs.fed.us (847-866-9311 x16)	Mark Rickenbach, Dept. For. Ecol. and Manage., Univ. of Wisconsin-Madison	mgrickenbach@ facstaff.wisc.edu (608-262-0134)
2003	Changing housing density in the rural Midwest	Robert Haight, NC-4803, St. Paul	rhaight@fs.fed.us (651-649-5178)	C. Montgomery, Oregon State Univ.	

(Table 1 continued on next page)

(Table 1 continued)

Year	Study title	NC contact(s)	NC contact info	Cooperator(s)	Cooperator contact info
2003	Water quality as an indicator of change in the Midwestern landscape	Thomas Crow, NC-4101, Grand Rapids	tcrow@fs.fed.us (218-326-7110)	Heidi Asbjornsen, Dept. Nat. Resour. Ecol. and Manage., Iowa State Univ.	hasbjorn@iastate.edu (515-294-7703)
2003	Ozone exposure response functions for predicting ecological risk to Midwestern forests	Warren Heilman, NC-4401, East Lansing	wheilman@fs.fed.us (517-355-7740 x27)	George Host, Nat. Resour. Res. Inst., Univ. of Minnesota-Duluth, David Mladenoff, Dept. For. Ecol. and Manage., Univ. of Wisconsin-Madison	ghost@umn.edu (218-720-4264), djmladen@facstaff. wisc.edu (608-262-1992)
2003	A model for sustaining natural resources in urban and urbanizing areas	John Dwyer, NC-4902, Evanston	jdwyer@fs.fed.us, (847-866-9311 x17)	David Nowak, NE Research Station-Syracuse	dnowak@fs.fed.us (315-448-3200)
2003	The implications of sprawl for resource management	John Dwyer, NC-4902, Evanston	jdwyer@fs.fed.us (847-866-9311 x17)	Gina Childs, NE Area, State and Private Forestry, St. Paul	gchilds@fs.fed.us (651-649-5296)
2003	Scenarios of landscape change effects on tropospheric ozone risk	Warren Heilman, NC-4401, East Lansing	wheilman@fs.fed.us (517-355-7740 x27)		

Table 2.—Landscape change publications and related products

Publications

1. Andersen, O.; Crow, T.R.; Lietz, S.M.; Stearns, F. 1996.
Transformation of a landscape in the upper mid-west, USA: the history of the lower St. Croix river valley, 1830 to present. Landscape and Urban Planning. 35: 247-267.

2. Austin, M.E. 2004.
Resident perspectives of the open space conservation subdivision in Hamburg Township, Michigan. Landscape and Urban Planning. 69: 245-253.

3. Austin, M.E.; Kaplan, R. 2003.
Resident involvement in natural resource management: open space conservation design in practice. Local Environment. 8(2): 141-154.

4. Bengston, D.N.; Fletcher, J.; Nelson, K.C. 2004.
Public policies for managing urban growth and protecting open space: policy instruments and lessons learned in the United States. Landscape and Urban Planning. 69: 271-286.

5. Bergen, K.M.; Brown, D.G.; Rutherford, J.; Gustafson, E. 2002.
Hotspots of land-cover change in the North-Central Region using USGS LUDA and NOAA AVHRR. In: Proceedings, IEEE IGARSS; 2002 June; Toronto.

6. Brawn, Jeffrey D.; Robinson, Scott K.; Thompson, Frank R., III. 2001.
The role of disturbance in the ecology and conservation of birds. Annual Review of Ecology and Systematics. 32: 251-276.

7. Brosofske, K.D.; Chen, J.; Crow, T.R.; Saunders, S.C. 1999.
Vegetation responses to landscape structure at multiple scales across a northern Wisconsin, USA, pine barrens landscape. Plant Ecology. 143: 203-218.

8. Brosofske, K.D.; Chen, J.; Crow, T.R. 2001.
Understory vegetation and site factors: implications for a managed Wisconsin landscape. Forest Ecology and Management. 146: 75-87.

9. Brown, D.G.; Duh, J.-D. 2004.
Spatial simulation for translating from land use to land cover. International Journal of Geographical Information Science. 18(1): 35-60.

10. Burhans, D.E.; Dearborn, D.; Thompson, F.R.; Faaborg, J. 2002.
Factors affecting predation at songbird nests in old fields. Journal of Wildlife Management. 66(1): 240-249.

11. Cifaldi, R.; Allan, J.D.; Duh, J.-D.; Brown, D.G. 2004.
Spatial patterns in land cover of exurbanizing watersheds in southeastern Michigan. Landscape and Urban Planning. 66: 107-123.

12. Crow, T.R.; Host, G.E.; Mladenoff, D.J. 1999.
Ownership and ecosystem as sources of spatial heterogeneity in a forested landscape, Wisconsin, USA. Landscape Ecology. 14: 449-463.

13. Dwyer, J.F.; Chavez, D.J. [In press].
The challenges of managing public lands on the wildland urban interface. In: Duryea, M.L.; Vince, S.W., eds. The wildland-urban interface: sustaining forests in a changing landscape. Gainesville, FL: University of Florida.

14. Dwyer, J.F.; Nowak, D.J.; Noble, M.H. 2003.
Sustaining urban forests. Journal of Arboriculture. 29(1): 49-55.

15. Dwyer, J.F.; Nowak, D.J.; Noble, M.H.; Sisinni, S.M. 2000.
Connecting people with ecosystems in the 21st century: an assessment of our nation's urban forests. Gen. Tech. Rep. PNW-GTR-490. Portland, OR: U.S. Department of Agriculture, Forest Service, Pacific Northwest Research Station. 493 p.

16. Fast, J.D.; Heilman, W.E. 2000.
Simulations of ozone in the Great Lakes Region. In: 24th conference on biometeorology and aerobiology; 2000 August 14-18; Davis, CA. Boston, MA: American Meteorological Society: 176-177.

17. Fast, J.D.; Heilman. W.E. 2002a.
The effect of lake temperatures and emissions on ozone exposure in the western Great Lakes region. Journal of Applied Meteorology. 42(9): 1197-1217.

18. Fast, J.D.; Heilman, W.E. 2002b.
The effect of lake temperatures on ozone in the western Great Lakes region. In: 25th conference on agricultural and forest meteorology; 2002 May 20-24; Norfolk, VA. Boston, MA: American Meteorological Society: J66-J67.

19. Fast, J.D.; Heilman, W.E.; Bian, X. 1998.
Weather patterns associated with high ozone concentrations in the Great Lakes Region. In: 23d conference on agricultural and forest meteorology; 1998 November 2-6; Albuquerque, NM. Boston, MA: American Meteorological Society: 333-336.

20. Gobster, P.H. 2001.
Visions of nature: compatibility and conflict in urban park restoration. Landscape and Urban Planning. 56(1-2): 35-51.

21. Gobster, P.H.; Hull, R.B. 2001.
Restoring nature: continuing the conversation. Ecological Restoration. 19(4): 225-226.

22. Gobster, P.H.; Hull, R.B., eds. 2000.
Restoring nature: perspectives from the social sciences and humanities. Washington, DC: Island Press. 320 p.

23. Gobster, P.H.; Rickenbach, M.G. 2004.
Private forestland parcelization and development in Wisconsin's Northwoods: perceptions of resource-oriented stakeholders. Landscape and Urban Planning. 69: 165-182.

24. Gobster, P.H.; Schmidt, T.L. 2000.
The use of amenity indicators in anticipating private forestland parcelization: a look at the Lake States' Northwoods. In: DeCoster, L., ed. Proceedings, Fragmentation 2000: a conference on sustaining private forests in the 21st century; 2000 September 17-20; Annapolis, MD. Alexandria, VA: The Sampson Group: 170-181.

25. Gobster, Paul H.; Haight, Robert G.; Shriner, Dave. 2000a.
Landscape change in the Midwest: an integrated research and development program. Journal of Forestry. 98(3): 9-14.

26. Gobster, P.H.; Haight, R.G.; Shriner, D.S. 2000b.
Integrated research on midwestern landscape change: a program description and progress report. In: DeCoster, L., ed. Proceedings, Fragmentation 2000: a conference on sustaining private forests in the 21st century; 2000 September 17-20; Annapolis, MD. Alexandria, VA: The Sampson Group: 375-382.

27. Gustafson, E.J.; Knutson, M.G.; Niemi, G.J.; Friberg, M.H. 2002.
Evaluation of spatial models to predict vulnerability of forest birds to brood parasitism by brown-headed cowbirds. Ecological Applications. 12(2): 412-426.

28. Hammer, R.B.; Stewart, S.I.; Winkler, R.; Radeloff, V.C.; Voss, P.R. 2004.
Characterizing spatial and temporal residential density patterns from 1940-1990 across the North Central United States. Landscape and Urban Planning. 69: 183-199.

29. Hull, R. Bruce; Gobster, Paul H. 2000.
Restoring forest ecosystems: the human dimension. Journal of Forestry. 98(8): 32-36.

30. Hull, R. Bruce; Stewart, Susan I. 2002.
Social consequence of change in the Urban Wildland Interface. In: Macie, Edward A.; Hermansen, L. Annie, eds. 2002 Human influences on forest ecosystems: the southern wildland-urban interface assessment. Gen. Tech. Rep. SRS-55. Asheville, NC: U.S. Department of Agriculture, Forest Service, Southern Research Station: 115-129.

31. Johnson, K.M. 2002.
The rural rebound of the 1990s and beyond. In: Levitt, James N., ed. Conservation in the Internet age: threats and opportunities. Washington, DC: Island Press: 63-82.

32. Johnson, K.M.; Stewart, S.I. 2001.
Recreation and amenity migration in urban proximate areas: report of survey results. Working Papers of Recreation and Amenity Migration Project. No. 1, 2001. Chicago, IL: Loyola University, Department of Socioloy and Anthropology. 47 p.

33. Kaplan, R.; Austin, M.E. 2004.
Out in the country: sprawl and the quest for nature nearby. Landscape and Urban Planning. 69: 235-243.

34. Kaplan, R.; Austin, M.E.; Kaplan, S. [In press].
Open space communities: resident perception, nature benefits, and terminological problems. Journal of the American Planning Association.

35. Marans, Robert W. 2003.
Understanding environmental quality through quality of life studies: the 2001 DAS and its use of subjective and objective indicators. Landscape and Urban Planning. 65: 73-83.

36. Pagen, R.W.; Thompson, F.R.; Burhans, D.E. 2001.
A comparison of point-count and mist-net detections of songbirds by habitat and time-of-season. Journal of Field Ornithology. 73(1): 53-59.

37. Peak, R.G. 2002.
Factors affecting avian species richness, density, and nest success in riparian corridors. Columbia, MO: University of Missouri-Columbia. 72 p. M.S. thesis.

38. Peak, R.G.; Thompson, F.R., III; Shaffer, T.L. 2004.
Factors affecting songbird nest survival in riparian forests in a Midwestern agricultural landscape. The Auk. 121(3): n.p.

39. Ribe, Robert G.; Armstrong, Edward T.; Gobster, Paul H. 2002.
Scenic vistas and the changing policy landscape: visualizing and testing the role of visual resources in ecosystem management. Landscape Journal. 21(1): 42-66.

40. Rickenbach, M.G.; Gobster, P.H. 2003.
Stakeholders' perceptions of parcelization in Wisconsin's Northwoods. Journal of Forestry. 101(6): 18-23.

41. Ruliffson, J.A.; Gobster, P.H.; Haight, R.G.; Homans, F.R. 2002.
Niches in the urban forest: organizations and their role in acquiring metropolitan open space. Journal of Forestry. 100(6): 16-23.

42. Ruliffson, J.A.; Haight, R.G.; Gobster, P.H.; Homans, F.R. 2003. *Metropolitan natural area protection to maximize public access and species representation.* Environmental Science and Policy. 6: 291-299.

43. Sabor, A.A.; Radeloff, V.C.; Hammer, R.B.; Stewart, S.I. 2003. *Relationships between housing density and timber harvest in the Upper Lake States.* In: Buse, L.J.; Perera, A.H., comps. Meeting emerging ecological, economic, and social challenges in the Great Lakes region: popular summaries. For. Res. Inf. Pap. 155. Sault Ste. Marie, ON: Ontario Ministry of Natural Resources, Ontario Forest Research Institute: 80-82.

44. Schmidt, T.L.; McWilliams, W.H. 2000. *Current status and trends of privately owned northern USA timberlands.* In: DeCoster, L., ed. Proceedings, Fragmentation 2000: a conference on sustaining private forests in the 21st century; 2000 September 17-20; Annapolis, MD. Alexandria, VA: The Sampson Group, Inc.: 64-72.

45. Schroeder, H.W. 2000. *What makes a place special? Interpretation of written survey responses in natural resource planning.* In: Bengston, D., ed. Applications of computer-aided text analysis in natural resources. Gen. Tech. Rep. NC-211. St. Paul, MN: U.S. Department of Agriculture, Forest Service, North Central Research Station: 7-11.

46. Schroeder, H.W. 2002. *Experiencing nature in special places.* Journal of Forestry. 100(5): 8-14.

47. Stewart, S.I. 2002. *Amenity migration.* In: Luft, K.; MacDonald, S., comps. Trends 2000: shaping the future, 5th Outdoor recreation and tourism trends symposium; 2000 September 17-20; Lansing, MI. East Lansing, MI: Michigan State University: 369-378.

48. Stewart, S.I.; Radeloff, V.C.; Hammer, R.B. 2003. *Characteristics and location of the Wildland-Urban Interface in the United States.* In: Proceedings, 2d International wildland fire ecology and fire management workshop; 2003 November 16-20; Orlando, FL. 6 p.

49. Stewart, W.P.; Liebert, D.; Larkin, K.W. 2004. *Community identities as visions for landscape change.* Landscape and Urban Planning. 69: 315-334.

50. Thompson, Frank R., III. 2000. *Fragmented Midwestern forests and songbird populations: where do we go from here?* In: McCabe, Richard E.; Loos, Samantha E., eds. Transactions of the 65th North American wildlife and natural resource conference; 2000 March 24-28; Rosemont, IL. Washington, DC: Wildlife Management Institute: 238-251.

51. Thompson, F.R.; Burhans, D.E. 2003. *Predation of songbird nests differs by predator and between field and forest habitats.* Journal of Wildlife Management. 67(2): 408-416.

52. Thompson, F.R., III; DeGraaf, R.M. 2001. *Conservation approaches for woody, early successional communities in the eastern United States.* Wildlife Society Bulletin. 29: 483-494.

53. Thompson, F.R.; Burhans, D.E.; Root, B. 2002. *Effects of point count protocol on bird abundance and variability estimates and power to detect population trends.* Journal of Field Ornithology. 73(2): 141-150.

54. Vigmostad, K.E. 2003. *Michigan real estate developer perspectives on development, sustainability, and nature: an autoethnography.* East Lansing, MI: Michigan State University. 130 p. Ph.D. dissertation.

55. Vogt, Christine A.; Marans, Robert W. 2002. *Understanding landscape change in open space neighborhoods: views from developers and residents.* In: Schuster, Rudy, comp., ed. Proceedings, 2002 Northeastern recreation research symposium; 2002 April 13-16; Bolton Landing, NY. Gen. Tech. Rep. NE-302. Newtown Square, PA: U.S. Department of Agriculture, Forest Service, Northeastern Research Station: 72-78.

56. Vogt, Christine A.; Marans, Robert W. 2001. *The role, use and benefits of natural recreation areas within and near residential subdivisions.* In: Todd, Sharon, ed. Proceedings, 2001 Northeastern recreation research symposium. Gen. Tech. Rep. NE-289. Newtown Square, PA: U.S. Department of Agriculture, Forest Service, Northeastern Research Station: 208-213.

57. Vogt, C.A.; Marans, R.W. 2003. *Open space neighborhoods: residents' views of new forms of development.* Journal of Park and Recreation Administration. 21(4): 49-69.

Related products

Juzwik, J.; Cook, S.; Haugen, L.; Elwell, J. 2004. *Oak wilt: people and trees—a community approach to management.* Gen. Tech. Rep. NC-240. St. Paul, MN: U.S. Department of Agriculture, Forest Service, North Central Research Station. CD-Rom version 2004 v 1.3.

Potts, R.S. 2003. *The changing midwest: an atlas of landscape change.* Available on line at: http://www.ncrs.fs.fed.us/

Table 3.—NCRS investments in landscape change research

Fiscal year	IP funds	RWU funds	Total NCRS	Leveraged funds	Total funding for FY
1999	$30,000	$403,636	$433,636	$289,115	$722,751
2000	$50,000	$910,676	$960,676	$738,610	$1,699,286
2001	$120,000	$778,888	$898,888	$564,817	$1,463,705
2002	$154,363	$659,569	$813,932	$391,490	$1,205,422
2003	$215,000	$637,356	$852,356	$501,014	$1,353,370
Total	$569,363	$3,390,125	$3,959,488	$2,485,046	$6,444,534

Table 4.—Partner organizations

For Profit
    InfoTrend
Government
    Department of Energy
        Battelle Pacific Northwest National
        Laboratory
    USDA Forest Service
     NE Area, State and Private Forestry
     Northeastern Research Station, Amherst
     Northeastern Research Station, Syracuse
     Pacific Southwest Research Station, Riverside
     Rocky Mountain Research Station
    USGS
Tribal
    Great Lakes Indian Wildlife and
    Fisheries Commission
University
    Clemson University
        Dept. Forest Resources
    Iowa State University
        Dept. Landscape Architecture
        Dept. Natural Resource Ecology and
        Management
    Loyola University Chicago
        Dept. Sociology and Anthropology
    Michigan State University
        Dept. Community, Agriculture, Recreation
        and Resource Studies
    Northern Michigan University
        Communications and Performance Studies
    Oregon State University
    Purdue University
        Dept. Forestry and Natural Resources
        Dept. Health and Kinesiology

State University of New York-Syracuse
    College of Environmental Science and Forestry
University of Idaho
    Dept. Landscape Architecture
University of Illinois at Urbana-Champaign
    Dept. Leisure Studies
    Human-Environment Research Laboratory
    Dept. Advertising
    Dept. Animal Biology
University of Michigan
    College of Architecture and Urban Planning
    School of Natural Resources & Environment
University of Minnesota
    Dept. Applied Economics
    Dept. Continuing Education
    Dept. Fisheries and Wildlife
    Dept. Forest Resources
    Dept. Plant Pathology
University of Minnesota-Duluth
    Natural Resources Research Institute
University of Missouri
    Dept. Fisheries and Wildlife
University of Tennessee
University of Utah
    David Eccles School of Business
University of Wisconsin-Madison
    Dept. Landscape Architecture
    Dept. Urban and Regional Planning
    Dept. Forest Ecology and Management
    Dept. Rural Sociology
University of Wisconsin-Milwaukee
    Dept. Geography
Virginia Tech
    Dept. of Forest Resources

MISSION STATEMENT

We believe the good life has its roots in clean air, sparkling water, rich soil, healthy economies and a diverse living landscape. Maintaining the good life for generations to come begins with everyday choices about natural resources. The North Central Research Station provides the knowledge and the tools to help people make informed choices. That's how the science we do enhances the quality of people's lives.